The Supply Story

The Supply Story:
Professional Substitutes in Education

edited by

Sheila Galloway
and
Marlene Morrison

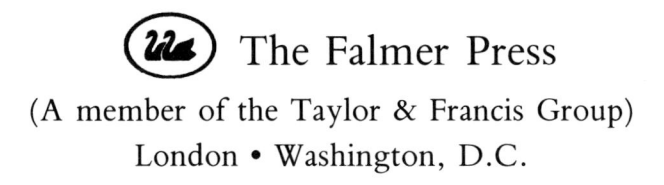

The Falmer Press

(A member of the Taylor & Francis Group)
London • Washington, D.C.

UK	The Falmer Press, 4 John Street, London WC1N 2ET
USA	The Falmer Press, Taylor & Francis Inc., 1900 Frost Road, Suite 101, Bristol, PA 19007

© S. Galloway and M. Morrison 1994

All rights reserved. No part of this publication may be reproduced, stored in a retrieval system, or transmitted in any form or by any means, electronic, mechanical, photocopying, recording or otherwise, without permission in writing from the Publisher.

First published in 1994

A catalogue record for this book is available from the British Library

Library of Congress Cataloging-in-Publication Data are available on request

ISBN 0 7507 0282 6 cased
ISBN 0 7507 0283 4 paper

Jacket design by Caroline Archer

Typeset in 11/13pt Bembo by
Graphicraft Typesetters Ltd., Hong Kong.

Printed in Great Britain by Burgess Science Press, Basingstoke on paper which has a specified pH value on final paper manufacture of not less than 7.5 and is therefore 'acid free'.

Contents

		Page
Foreword		vii
Preface		ix
List of Figures and Tables		xi
List of Acronyms		xii

Chapter 1	Teacher Substitution: A Focal Point for Multiple Perspectives S. Galloway and M. Morrison	1
Part 1:	The Employee: Supply Teachers	15
Chapter 2	Celebrating Experience K. Green	16
Chapter 3	Highlighting a Grey Area M. Mullett	31
Chapter 4	Temps in the Classroom: A Case of Hidden Identities? M. Morrison	43
Part 2:	The Employment Context: Schools	67
Chapter 5	From Where I Stand: A Headteacher's Account M. Newton	68
Chapter 6	Square Pegs and Round Holes: The Supply Coordinator's Role in Employing and Deploying Staff S. Galloway	82

v

Contents

Chapter 7	Then and Now: Supply Teaching in the Infant School *C. Knight*	108
Part 3:	The Employer in Different Guises	121
Chapter 8	Human Resource Management: An LEA Response *P. Buzzing*	122
Chapter 9	The Language of Supply: A Shifting Interface for LEAs, Schools and Supply Teachers *M. Morrison*	137
Chapter 10	Supply Teaching as a Labour Market Phenomenon *R.M. Lindley*	157
Chapter 11	Conclusion: Confronting Paradox *S. Galloway and M. Morrison*	181
Appendixes		189
Notes on Contributors		196
Index		198

Foreword

Teachers and teaching have always been major subjects of research enquiry by policy makers, educational researchers, sociologists and economists among many others. This should hardly be surprising given that some 0.4 million people work as teachers in our schools.

A range of questions can be posed about the recruitment, supply and composition of the teaching force, about the age, gender and ethnicity of teachers. In short, much can be learned about the characteristics of teachers which is of use to policy makers and researchers. In turn, sociologists and educational researchers have been concerned to explore who becomes teachers, the ways in which they are socialized and the work which they do and we have acquired a greater understanding of teachers' lives and teachers' work from quantitative and qualitative studies.

Yet despite all this work, gaps still remain. One group of teachers about which we have relatively little knowledge are those who engage in 'supply work'. These teachers act as substitutes for permanent staff during periods of ill health or absence from school when other educational demands are made upon their time. But who are these supply teachers? What are their characteristics? What work do they take on and what is their experience of teaching? What contribution do they make to the teaching and learning experience?

Such a range of questions can be examined from a number of different perspectives. The role of LEAs and schools in recruiting supply teachers, the experience of supply teaching and the role of the supply teacher in the changing organizational structure of the school are all important areas for research and critical evaluation. In this volume, Sheila Galloway and Marlene Morrison have brought together a range of contributors who between them can provide a variety of stories about supply teachers and supply teaching. Among the contributors are researchers from economics, sociology and education as well as those who work with supply teachers. The result is a rich body of material that adds a new dimension to our understanding of teachers' lives, careers and work. At the heart of the volume is a series

Foreword

of essays by the editors on supply teachers' work which comes from a two-year research project they conducted in two local education authorities. All together these essays shed light on an important group of teachers whose experiences have been hidden from view. In this sense, the volume provides an important starting point for future research and policy making on a group of teachers who play an important part in the changing culture of our schools.

>Robert G. Burgess
>
>Director of CEDAR
>University of Warwick

Preface

In the late 1980s our research in a number of different educational settings revealed many varieties of 'supply situation'. Projects on teachers' in-service training, school development planning, curriculum evaluation and library use drew attention in different ways to supply issues as being crucial in the day-to-day life of schools, teachers and pupils. A two-year research project on supply teaching confirmed that matters relating to teacher substitution were central to teaching and learning processes, but that the concerns of those involved varied widely.

A preoccupation with gender and education persisted for both of us from earlier work on part-time women students and lecturers, and on class and gender distinctions in vocational education. Studying supply teachers (of whom the majority are women) juxtaposes issues related to educational provision with matters such as professional gender imbalances and women's careers; career breaks and the return to employment; and domestic support systems and childcare. Undoubtedly the backcloth to supply teaching is the wider perspective of women's working lives. However it must be recognized that there are also male supply teachers, and the treatment of supply in this book allows for this. Researching teacher substitution has made it increasingly clear that views of supply teachers are contradictory, paradoxical and expressed from a multitude of different positions.

Despite this, there has been a publications void. In this intriguing field, educational issues of professionalism and quality combine with those of social equality, but few attempts have been made to articulate the themes. Little research has been done but to anyone working in schools, it is apparent that the scarcity of written discussion has not been matched by silence from interested parties. On the contrary: opinions proliferate. Doing justice to such variety requires not just a 'mapping the territory' exercise. It also has to represent a kaleidoscope of ideological standpoints, professional expertise and personal opinion. This book takes a multidisciplinary approach, drawing on contributions from trainers, teachers, managers, researchers and others to articulate some of those differing perspectives. It is a collaborative venture in

Preface

which our own research, having provided the impetus and a link through each section of the book, is complemented by six further contributions which deal with the supply teaching phenomenon in rather different ways. The mix of material from research and practitioner sources conveys some part of the myriad of purposes, priorities, mechanisms and experience that constitute the supply scene. From alternative viewpoints the chapters explore the systems, structures and relationships associated with supply teaching or teacher substitution. This shared platform is provided to stimulate debate and allow readers to cross-reference from one area to another, drawing ideas and suggestions to fit their own needs and interests. Though the chapters differ as described, what they share is authenticity in their individual fields, which derives from their separate understanding and experience, whether it be based in research or practice.

If there is a voice that is under-represented, it is the direct voice of the supply teacher herself or himself. That body of information requires a different book. However, several contributions do take us through the door of the classroom, to the heart of what is involved in supply teaching, and to that extent the material takes the first step towards making visible an area of professional expertise that has been markedly ignored by policy-makers and researchers.

Finally we should like to thank a number of people and organizations who have helped in the preparation of this book. We should like to acknowledge the support of The Leverhulme Trust which funded the research project entitled 'Supply Teaching in English Schools: An Investigation of Policy, Processes and People'. We appreciate the responses provided by LEAs and teacher associations, and our thanks go to the teachers, pupils and others who remain anonymous but who shared their time, their thoughts and their classrooms with us.

Particular thanks go to Robert Burgess, Director of The Centre for Educational Development, Appraisal and Research, both for his involvement in the research project on supply teaching and continued interest in, and support of, the preparation of this book, and to the authors of individual chapters who have spent time discussing supply issues with us. Barbara Muldowney has given us unfailingly cheerful secretarial support. Any errors or omissions are our own.

                            Sheila Galloway
                            Marlene Morrison

                            Centre for Educational Development,
                            Appraisal and Research,
                            University of Warwick, 1993.

List of Figures and Tables

		Page
Figure 1	School-supply Links	91
Table 1	Functional Relocation in Education	160
Table 2	Re-orientation of External and Internal Labour Markets for School Teachers	161
Table 3	Staff Training Relating to Schools	165
Table 4	Job Content and School Occupational Structures	166

List of Acronyms

BTEC	Business and Technology Education Council
CEDAR	Centre for Educational Development, Appraisal and Research
CPVE	Certificate of Pre-Vocational Education
GCSE	General Certificate of Secondary Education
GEST	Grants for Educational Support and Training
GRIST	Grant-Related In-Service Training
INSET	In-Service Training
ITT	Initial Teacher Training
KITS	Keeping in Touch with Teaching and Supply Teacher Support
LEA	Local Education Authority
ROA	Records of Achievement
SACRE	Standing Advisory Council on Religious Education
TASC	Teaching as a Career Initiative
TRIST	TVEI-Related In-Service Training
TVEI	Technical and Vocational Education Initiative

Chapter 1

Teacher Substitution: A Focal Point for Multiple Perspectives

Sheila Galloway and Marlene Morrison

The Supply Story is, as so many titles are, something of a misnomer. There is no single supply story: as this volume demonstrates, there is a wide range of accounts, reflecting diverse perspectives on supply teaching. The aim of this book is to set some of these views alongside each other.

Our definition of a supply situation is any occasion when the regular (timetabled) teacher is not able to teach a scheduled class, and another adult is called on to teach or supervise these pupils. This view of teacher substitution includes internal as well as external cover. 'Supply teachers', however, are those who are employed on an occasional or temporary, short-term basis. They may work in one school or many. Some are able to work almost full-time in this way, yet do not have a regular contract with any employer or institution. Others work only infrequently. Teachers who hold part-time contracts may also do some supply work from time to time. There are still some teachers employed full-time as part of an LEA team, who are allocated to schools by the authority (and therefore have no option to refuse to work in any school which needs them). Finally, the development of (non-LEA) agencies has produced further diversity.

Teacher Substitution in Different Contexts

The very existence of qualified substitute teachers signals sophisticated education provision. In countries still working to establish a national education service staffed by professionally qualified people, the ability to draw sporadically on a pool of alternative teachers may seem an indulgence only possible in better-resourced systems. Elsewhere, cultural attitudes shape teachers' terms and conditions of employment, teaching methods and assumptions about pupil conduct. In Japan, for instance, maternity leave or teacher secondment will require a replacement teacher, but it is not unusual for pupils to continue working from textbooks in the absence of their teacher. Apart from post-sixteen groups, this is to date a strategy almost unknown in Britain.

Teacher absence has always been difficult for schools, partly in English education because of the *in loco parentis* role of the teacher. Partly also because instructional aims and pedagogical patterns traditionally make the regular teacher crucial to continuity of learning. New directions being explored in some schools may reduce the effects of teacher absence: adopting a facilitating role, and encouraging self-supported learning. One suspects nevertheless that the notion of classes 'on automatic pilot' as an agreed solution to cover difficulties would not be generally acceptable.

During the late 1980s, teacher absence for in-service training grew in an unprecedented way, making questions of teacher substitution a real concern in many schools. Reasons for this rapid expansion of training are explored in Burgess *et al.*, (1993) and McBride (1989). Programmes aimed at improving the quality of the teaching force were developed, often in relation to specific educational initiatives or legislation. Some provided opportunities for training to all teachers in service, others required certain postholders to attend in-service events. The most important early programme was TVEI-Related In-Service Training (TRIST), subsequently incorporated into Grant-Related In-Service Training (GRIST). Educational Support Grants (ESG) were also drawn into the development of the Grants for Educational Support and Training (GEST) scheme in the 1990s. An unprecedented range of training was available, intended ultimately to benefit pupils. The immediate effect, however, was to remove teachers from classes, making substitutes necessary, usually in the form of 'supply teachers'.

Training related to the Educational Reform Act (1988) and early implementation of the National Curriculum maintained the momentum. Even as Local Education Authorities (LEAs) adjusted to their new roles, school-focused training (often now school-based training) still took regular teachers away from their classes. Attempts to minimize teacher absence did not wholly resolve the situation. Only the impact of financial stringency and the local management of schools reduced the level of external supply cover.

Along with training, other reasons for teacher absence included illness, with stress-related causes increasing during this period (Dunham, 1992). School staff were also giving greater attention to public relations and liaison work, with associated primary or secondary schools, with educational support agencies, with industrial concerns, and with local communities. By the end of the 1980s the discontinuity to children's learning resulting from teacher absence was widely seen to be critical. In addition, while supply teachers could be found, they too rarely had the chance of any continued training geared to their own needs.

By the end of the 1980s some LEAs had noted the need to provide professional development opportunities for these teachers in reserve. One-off sessions, short courses and newsletters were relatively low-cost forms of support for what was essentially a changing population since many supply teachers would subsequently seek permanent posts. Unlike regular teachers, they attended training in their own time, and were not paid (accepting the potential loss of earnings when they were unavailable to work). They did not incur costs by leaving classes to be covered. Where training was available to supply teachers it was generally funded from allocations of GEST funding, with returners' schemes the main channel. There are, nonetheless, distinctions to be made between the needs of returners and those of supply teachers, however much the two groups may overlap.

Present trends are that the need for training for permanent staff will continue as successive phases of the National Curriculum are implemented. Supply teachers need to be professionally up-to-date as much as those they replace, and their working situations call for high classroom management skills. They have, however, no contractual relationship with LEA or school, and therefore no job security (except in the case of the very few remaining full-time 'team' members retained by some LEAs, and those permanent part-time teachers who chose to work extra hours on a supply basis). The curtailed role of LEAs means that in the 1990s responsibility for supply matters lies almost wholly with schools. Vetting procedures and salary payments remain with LEAs but many have disbanded or sharply restricted existing arrangements for training and support of substitute teachers. In 1993 GEST funding for women returners ceased, such schemes being perceived as less of a priority since teacher shortages appeared in the short-term to have eased. A long-term view would, however, indicate that this could be only a temporary respite. There is still no clearly articulated response to the supply teaching situation at national level.

Looking forward, developments will have to move on despite this policy vacuum which has persisted regardless of warnings from various sources. The House of Commons Education, Science and Arts Committee reporting in 1990 on the supply of teachers for the 1990s, successive reports of the Interim Advisory Committee on School Teachers Pay and Conditions (Great Britain House of Commons, Chilver Committee, 1990, 1991), and statements such as Her Majesty's

Inspectorate's report on teacher supply in seventeen schools (DES, 1990) all noted the importance of retraining and effectively deploying supply staff. Professional associations voiced concerns about supply teacher availability and quality. (e.g., AMMA *et al.*, 1990). Those LEAs which did produce guidance on supply issues were drawing attention to the importance that they attached to providing professional substitutes.

Supply teaching is a recognized route back into full-time teaching and the supply of teachers draws heavily on re-entrants. Since 1985 re-entrants have filled around 50 per cent or more of new appointments, exceeding newly trained teachers. In 1991 52 per cent of new appointments were returners to teaching (School Teachers' Review Body, 1993). Yet it appears unlikely that at national level more generous resources for supply teacher training will be seen as justifiable against central educational objectives.

The issues remain critical for pupils and teachers alike. What signs are there of possible future directions? Warning signs are reported of cost-cutting measures in schools where supply provision has been reduced. At the same time, in the absence of national and LEA impetus, some schools and consortia are experimenting with small-scale support for supply staff, even being prepared to pay regular supply teachers to attend training sessions. Such examples are important statements in all sorts of ways, not least in signalling the value that is put on good supply staff in some places. Training provided by an institution for those who work there occasionally will inevitably differ from that which would have been provided by a self-help group formed on the initiative of supply teachers themselves, or, by an LEA. Another alternative is for LEAs to offer training the cost of which is met by the individual, that is the supply teacher or returner and more examples of this may appear in coming years. The development of supply teaching agencies introduces new possibilities. Will such organizations take on a training role? In an evolving education market, we have yet to see what exactly the role of private teacher employment agencies will be (Hulme, 1993).

Research on Supply Teaching

Previous research on supply teaching has been limited, tending to pinpoint problematic elements of substitution. Earley (1986) identified some basic concerns about supply cover, while Mullett's (1989a) survey for one LEA gave useful information about supply teachers' attitudes. Loveys (1988) provided an authentic first-hand account of his own experience as a supply teacher. There are methodological difficulties to be faced in researching under such circumstances, as this writer admitted, but the access afforded by his work in a range of schools made a detailed analysis possible of certain features of supply teaching. Among these, he articulated some assumptions made in relation to gender. Connor's (1989) investigation (also available as Connor, 1993) assessed the impact of cover related to INSET in four secondary schools, using information from substitution sheets alongside interview data. From a long-term study of teacher identities, Nias (1989) explored material on temporary, part-time and supply teachers.

Moving away from individual concerns, Brown and Earley (1990) reviewed the management of cover situations again in the context of increasing levels of INSET. Taking a problem-solving approach, this report aimed to highlight ways of minimizing cover, focusing at LEA rather than at school or classroom level. In a very different context, a broad research project on classroom management was the impetus for Trotter and Wragg's (1990) study of supply teaching. Interviews with twenty teachers centred on how they saw their work, and first encounters with unfamiliar classes. In addition, teachers were invited to respond to photographs showing disruptive classroom situations. This study stressed the importance both of being prepared and of seeming to be prepared. Though experienced teachers brought typificatory knowledge to their supply work, they lacked knowledge about particular pupils and this made their work difficult.

Shilling (1990, 1991a and 1991b) all explored supply themes. A review of the literature sets out the role of the supply teacher in the 1990s, and assessed features of this work, described as:

> a highly demanding form of labour which offers participants little job satisfaction, control over their work or career prospects. (Shilling, 1991b, p. 6)

The motivation of supply teachers was explored: the author identified from the literature eight reasons why people embark on this type of teaching, in addition to the generally accepted aim of some women teachers to combine family responsibilities with paid work.

In Shilling 1990 and 1991a agency nursing was compared with supply teaching: a comparative case study of cover arrangements in one local education authority and one district health authority permitted the analysis of issues such as the motivation and domestic contexts of these occasional workers, the ways in which these affect their continued work, and structural features of the support system in both organizations.

Galloway (1993b)[1] indicated that alongside these reports, there are other publications which markedly ignored supply themes, and drew attention to the continuing non-appearance of teacher substitution in the literature: invisibility is a key feature. Morrison (1993) analysed how the curriculum is interpreted and delivered, and the part played in this by supply staff. Developing methodological themes, Morrison and Galloway (forthcoming) discuss researching transitory and fleeting relationships. Observation and diary data allow for the exploration of how the actors see reality in different ways.

Teacher substitution has both educational and sociological elements, and research findings therefore interest different audiences in different ways. No theory promises to encompass enough of the field, but we would argue that central areas of interest are those of power and visibility, both in terms of systems and structures, and also as evident in interactions between people and groups. However, other important concepts vie for attention: gender; time; work, employment and unpaid work; professionalism and training; career patterns. Both private and public worlds are relevant: the personal and the professional often overlap. Supply teaching as a theme raises diverse educational issues and impinges on almost every area of school life and beyond.

A number of conceptual themes can be explored in relation to supply teaching. Macro-level sociological theory has the potential to explain national policy as it is conveyed through to the schools, and it is clear that a systems approach can help in documenting how school organization and structures operationalize supply cover. Yet it is evident that restricting the analysis to structural features would be inadequate in studying those who are located mostly outside formal systems and structures. Here Lukes (1974) proves valuable in identifying the contribution of those whose very invisibility has kept their job from being recognized as an appropriate area for research, and has perhaps also kept their interests from being articulated. His analysis of decision-making and non-decision-making, and of the ways in which certain themes are either manipulated out of agenda or never even articulated can help to inform research planning and thinking. This analysis offers useful ways into a study of teacher substitution. The presentation of choice and of latent conflict alerts us to the need to be sceptical about observable conflict, and to the value of asking about alternatives: 'One can take steps to find out what it is that people would have done otherwise' (p. 50). (It is in the work with supply teachers as individuals that these ideas have proved most fruitful.)

A Focal Point for Multiple Perspectives

In other ways too, while macro-level decisions in national policy on supply can be assessed, it is evident that the key processes relating to supply are frequently interactions between particular people and groups. The teaching and learning taking place is not adequately understood unless time is given to tracing through micro-level negotiation and decision-making. This is demonstrated by interactionist studies and particularly the tradition of school ethnography such as Lacey (1970), Hargreaves, D. (1967), Hargreaves, A. (1986), Ball (1981), Burgess (1983) and King (1978). Research of this type convinces of its authenticity by attention to detail, by using a range of research techniques, by presenting multiple perspectives, and by collecting data over a long time-scale at the micro-level. If grounds for generalization are more limited, the strength of these texts lies in identifying critical processes and the development of models that others may chose to take further. As our own research shows, a multi-site study operates on a different time-scale but can also illuminate key processes.

Gender Perspectives

Gender is more than just an important theme but does not provide an over-riding frame for analysis. In a profession which is still male-dominated at senior management and administrative levels, yet where women predominate numerically, the supply teacher can be said to typify socio-economic features of a gendered profession even more markedly than the teachers in permanent full-time employment. Most of the women doing supply work would be in more secure employment were it not for family responsibilities. Whether their choices were 'free' or not is debatable. Our research offers evidence of a woman teacher returning home in the lunch hour to care for an elderly parent, a single parent balancing earning money during term-time against spending summer days with her pre-school child, a mother of a handicapped child whose attempt to return to teaching is constrained by the state of his health. It is not the purpose of this volume to use supply teaching to treat the wider issues of gender, but they do inform our thinking in the selection of material for this book.

However, there are also male supply teachers such as the freelance writer doing occasional supply work, the father responsible for the care of two children under seven whose wife works full-time, and retired men in both primary and secondary phases. This warns against an unduly simplified reading of gender issues, and confirms the need for a wider brief. A book on supply teaching inevitably puts women's experience centre-stage, and in documenting school mechanisms for cover, professional judgments about specialist skills as against 'good all-round' teaching expertise, and giving attention to the personal experience of supply teachers, critical features of the role of the woman teacher become apparent, not least in the concerns and priorities of those returners who choose the supply route back to teaching.

Much is gained by a wider view, from the macro- to the most micro-level investigation, and by exploiting an eclectic range of concepts, methods and data as elements of an overall scheme which allows the coherent exploration of different areas. In similar vein, the contributions to this volume offer the chance to explore further specific themes.

The Organization of the Book

Part 1 presents material that draws on the perspectives of the individual supply teacher reflecting on career breaks, returning to work, and in the primary classroom. Part 2 moves to the institutional context within which they work, that is secondary and primary schools. Part 3 considers employment contexts beyond the school setting. The fundamental nature of current educational change colours the three chapters in this section most sharply, but it is apparent in different ways throughout the book.

After Chapter 1 which is an introduction to the book, Part 1 Chapter 2 gives a teacher educator's perspective on how aspects of a career break contribute to the professional understanding of those returning to classroom teaching. While the career break is frequently said to result in loss of confidence, this chapter defines a strength of supply teachers as the ability to bring to their teaching an awareness of children's lives outside the classroom. Weaving her own response to students on her course with data from a programme of interviews, Kath Green includes methodological comment, and demonstrates the value put by returning teachers on their out-of-school knowledge. Yet this is rarely acknowledged, and the chapter also indicates some of the hurdles facing supply teachers who seek full-time work. Chapter 3 relates how a 'self-help' support group grew out of the professional concerns of supply teachers in the mid-1980s. This grassroots activity gained recognition from the LEA, attracting support and financial resourcing. Mary Mullett reports on a small-scale survey conducted for the LEA, which remains one of the few (statistical) sources of evidence on supply teachers. Her own role took on a training and liaison brief, but the chapter's conclusion sounds a salutary note in current financial circumstances. Chapter 4 presents an in-depth analysis of supply teaching in action. Marlene Morrison juxtaposes the sometimes contradictory expectations of permanent staff with the experience of supply teachers, to examine the images that predominate and the ways in which teachers' identities are sustained.

In Part 2, Chapter 5 features the educational and financial judgments made in a 12–18 comprehensive school. Malcolm Newton explains the priorities on which his staff operate, the school cover policy, and describes the school's model of supply use. In Chapter 6 Sheila Galloway's case study shows how macro-level initiatives intertwine at the micro-level with school priorities and local emergencies. The supply coordinator juggles the professional competences of available teachers against the lessons needing cover, seeking both to provide specialist teaching and to protect pupils' continuity of learning, while maintaining staff morale. In Chapter 7, Cynthia Knight writes from experience as a class teacher and advisory teacher when she participated in training herself including the provision of INSET sessions dependent on supply cover. As a deputy and now a headteacher of a city primary school she engages supply staff and makes judgments about expenditure on cover. The chapter narrates yet another supply 'story' but it also documents fluctuating educational trends in a wider sense, not least in sketching in the potential role of supply teacher agencies.

Moving to the employer's standpoint in Part 3, the final three chapters reflect several forms of educational change. Pauline Buzzing's work with women returners is the basis of a discussion of supply teaching as a route for returners. Chapter 8 shows how West Sussex LEA invested in training and support programmes and this early work was taken up by national organizations. It also assesses the effect of the removal of GEST funding. In the early 1990s employers' policies were framed in distinctive terms. In Chapter 9 Marlene Morrison reviews the discourse that shaped such statements about teacher substitution, taking issue with some common assumptions, and the chapter sounds a warning note on the security of employment of permanent staff. This is taken forward in Chapter 10's labour market analysis of supply teaching as an example of the generic phenomenon of qualified people doing temporary work. Robert Lindley discusses the nature of the employment relationship and the distinction between internal and external labour market policies. The location of teaching within the occupational–organizational–industrial structure can shift in response to changes in the socio-economic environment: the chapter considers some implications of this and looks to the future.

The various chapters differ in style because practitioners, researchers, trainers, teachers and educational consultants have their own discourses. The hope is that this collection can be a catalyst in provoking discussion, and we can learn from the tone of these voices just as we learn from the substance. In the concluding chapter we trace through the varying perspectives of the several contributions, and identify key concerns, outlining some of the complex educational and sociological issues integral to 'the supply story'. The conclusion incorporates issues for individuals, for schools, for LEAs, and for national policy.

Recurring Themes

Each chapter covers an identifiable spectrum of interest: one focuses on labour market themes, another on women's personal experience and related research issues. Others define and redefine notions of professionalism. While some chapters report on managing supply in comfortable, sought-after areas where substitute teachers might well wish to work, others record the situation in inner-city schools, where unemployment is high and fewer pupils have English as their first language. Examples are given of an authority-led initiative and one where the LEA became involved in supporting the organic growth of a 'grassroots' group. The transitional role of the LEA is apparent in several chapters, particularly those in Part 3. Other transitions are noted: for instance school governors, learning how best to manage their own budgets, while the loss of GEST funding takes supply teachers further away from the possibility of training. We see how voluntary groups develop into networks initially from the interest and commitment of particular people, but rely for their continuance upon official patronage. Employment issues are explored theoretically and in references to job applications and career breaks. The appearance of private agencies and 'freelance' teachers links Parts 2 and 3. Where staffing policies and re-entry arise in Part 1, related themes are discussed from different perspectives at the end of the book.

Part 2 highlights matters of teaching and learning and distinctions recur between the less desirable strategies of 'containment', 'babysitting', 'childminding' and the 'holding operation', and the interactive approach that constitutes 'real' teaching. What is the contribution of supply staff and how should schools validate their work? We see supply teachers deployed not just to cover classes but also to enrich the curriculum, both personally and by releasing permanent staff for training. Concerns about status, reception and identity that appeared in Part 1 are recalled

A Focal Point for Multiple Perspectives

in later examples and prefigure the reference in Part 3 to work done with supply teachers being 'binnable'. Finally, the overlap between supply teachers and returners is rightly reflected in several contributions but we are also reminded that the supply teaching workforce includes many people who are not women returners.

If the purpose of researching supply teaching is to understand, explain and learn from teacher substitution, it is equally important to put it on the educational agenda. Such matters already have a place on the feminist agenda, but they need to be more widely discussed. Finally, understanding supply teaching can illuminate any study of educational power structures and relationships, as well as extending our thinking about teaching and learning processes.

Note

1 This article and the two following were part of the research project 'Supply Teaching in English Schools: an investigation of policy, processes and people'. This was funded by The Leverhulme Trust and conducted in 1991 and 1992 by R. Burgess, S. Galloway and M. Morrison at the Centre for Educational Development, Appraisal and Research at the University of Warwick.

References

AMMA, NAHT, NASUWT, NUT, PAT, and SHA (1990) *Report of Joint Union Survey on Teacher Shortages: September 1990*, London, Jevons Brown.
BALL, S.J. (1981), *Beachside Comprehensive: A case study of secondary schooling*, Cambridge, Cambridge University Press.
BLACKBURNE, L., ARKIN, A. and HACKETT, G. (1989) 'Poorly paid and powerless', *Times Educational Supplement*, 6 October.
BROWN, S. and EARLEY, P. (1990) *Enabling Teachers to Undertake Inservice Education and Training*, Slough, NFER for the DES.
BURGESS, R.G. (1983), *Experiencing Comprehensive Education*, London, Methuen.
BURGESS, R.G., CONNOR, J., GALLOWAY, S., MORRISON, M. and NEWTON, M. (1993) *Implementing Teachers' In-Service Education and Training*, London, The Falmer Press.
CONNOR, J. (1989) *Implementing INSET: A Case Study of one LEA*, CEDAR Report No.3.
CONNOR, J. (1993) 'INSET and the issue of disruption in secondary schools' in BURGESS, R.G. *et al.*, *Implementing Teachers' In-Service Education and Training*, London, The Falmer Press.
DES (1990) *Teacher Supply in Seventeen Schools in Tower Hamlets and Wandsworth*, A Report by HMI, HMSO. 159/90/DS.

DUNHAM, J. (1992) *Stress in Teaching* (2nd edition), London, Routledge.
EARLEY, P. (1986) *Questions of Supply: An Exploratory Study of External Cover Arrangements*, Slough, NFER.
GALLOWAY, S. (1993b) '"Out of Sight, Out of Mind": A response to the literature on supply teaching', in *Educational Research*, 35, 2, pp. 159–69.
GREAT BRITAIN HOUSE OF COMMONS (Education, Science and Arts Committee) (1990) *Second Report of the Committee on the Supply of Teachers for the 1990s*, Vol.1, London, HMSO.
GREAT BRITAIN HOUSE OF COMMONS (Interim Advisory Committee) (1990) *Third Report of the IAC on Schoolteachers' Pay and Conditions (Chair: Lord Chilver)*, London, HMSO, 30 January.
GREAT BRITAIN HOUSE OF COMMONS (Interim Advisory Committee) (1991) *Fourth Report of the IAC on Schoolteachers' Pay and Conditions*, (Chair: Lord Chilver), London, HMSO, 18 January.
HARGREAVES, A. (1986) *Two Cultures of Schooling: the Case of Middle Schools*, Lewes, The Falmer Press.
HARGREAVES, D. (1967) *Social relations in a Secondary School*, London, Routledge and Kegan Paul.
HULME, J. (1993) 'Supply and Demand', in *The Teacher*, May/June, pp. 12–14
KING, R. (1978) *All Things Bright and Beautiful? A Sociological Study of Infants' Classrooms*, Chichester, Wiley.
LACEY, C. (1970) *Hightown Grammar*, Manchester, Manchester University Press.
LOVEYS, M. (1988) 'Supplying the Demand? Contract, mobility, and institutional location in the changing world of the supply teacher' in OZGA, J. (Ed.) *School Work: Approaches to the Labour Process of Teaching*, Milton Keynes, Open University Press.
LUKES, S. (1974) *Power: A Radical View*, London, Macmillan.
MCBRIDE, R. (Ed.) (1989) *The In-Service Training of Teachers*, Lewes, The Falmer Press.
MORRISON, M. (1993) 'Running for Cover: Substitute Teaching and the Secondary Curriculum', in *Curriculum*, 14, 2, pp. 125–39.
MORRISON, M. and GALLOWAY, S. (forthcoming) 'Researching Moving Targets: using diaries to explore supply teachers' lives', paper presented at the British Sociological Association Annual Conference, University of Essex, April 1993, to be published in the collection of selected conference papers.
MULLETT, M. (1989a) 'Research into primary supply teacher issues: results and report', Buckinghamshire County Council, Aylesbury Education Department, July.
NIAS, J. (1989) *Primary Teachers Talking: A Study of Teaching as Work*, London, Routledge.
SHILLING, C. (1990) 'The organization of supply workers in state schools and the National Health Service: a comparison', in *Journal of Education Policy*, 5, 2, pp. 127–41.

SHILLING, C. (1991a) 'Permanent supports or temporary props? Supply workers in state schools and the National Health Service', in *Gender and Education*, 3, 1, pp. 61–80.
SHILLING, C. (1991b) 'Supply Teachers: working on the margins: A Review of the Literature', in *Educational Research*, 33, 1, Spring, pp. 3–11.
SCHOOL TEACHERS' REVIEW BODY (1993) *School Teachers' Review Body: Second Report* (CM 2151) London, HMSO.
TROTTER, A. and WRAGG, E. (1990) 'A Study of Supply Teachers', in *Research Papers in Education*, 5, 3, pp. 251–76.

Part 1

The Employee: Supply Teachers

Chapter 2

Celebrating Experience

Kath Green

The authors of later chapters seek in different ways to make visible the experiences of supply teachers and teaching. In this first chapter the author makes these visible by celebrating women's experience within and beyond classrooms. Career breaks are frequently referred to as times of breakdown in confidence and skills. In contrast, this chapter makes positive links between personal experiences during breaks in service, and subsequent teaching strategies. The need to make connections is made more urgent by what the author views as a silent, creeping devaluation of experience. In the absence of formal policy statements, personal and professional experiences become expensive commodities for managers seeking to make savings on school budgets. Rejecting deficit models of supply teachers' work, the author takes an uncompromising stance in asserting the 'side' we need to be 'on' in affirming rather than devaluing the personal *and* professional experience of women teachers. She draws on experience as a leader of courses for supply teachers and returners.

Career Breaks and Professional Development

In the current educational climate, experienced teachers are rapidly becoming an endangered species. As more and more schools take responsibility for managing their own budgets and the budgets to be managed are pared to the bone, there is a real danger that the maxim 'cheapest is best' will apply to an increasing number of staff appointments. Listening to a number of headteachers and to student teachers returning from interviews across the country, it is quite clear that appointment committees no longer feel free to appoint the person whose range of experience best fits the school's current needs. All too often the pressure is there to appoint the cheapest teacher.

At present, those teachers particularly at risk are women teachers wanting to return to the classroom after a career break. Their previous teaching experience, together with the additional experience of bringing up children, risks being devalued at a stroke. In my current role as course leader of a 'Women Returners' course for primary teachers I am constantly struck by the wealth of additional experience which these returners bring with them on their return to the classroom and in recent years I have engaged in research in a deliberate attempt to validate their experiences.

Initially, my investigations arose out of my involvement with a supply teachers' retraining course based at Nottingham Polytechnic. (This and the returners' courses have been funded at various times by the Training Agency, Nottinghamshire LEA and most recently Nottingham Trent University.) During the interviewing process for the course, I was struck by the very positive view taken by interviewees of their life experiences *during* their career breaks and how they appeared to see these experiences as an important part of their professional development.

This certainly matched my own experience where I viewed my own career break as a time of tremendous professional growth enabling me to gain real insight into young children's early development, together with first-hand knowledge of the parental perspective in education. Not untypically, this period included involvement in a wide range of voluntary activities and organizations. I was a post-natal supporter for the National Childbirth Trust which involved visiting young mothers after the birth of a baby in order to offer support, and was struck, then, by the powerful feelings of isolation and anxiety being experienced by many of these mothers. Subsequently, I met with other mothers at 'mother and toddler groups' and later became involved in the pre-school playgroup movement both as a parental helper and trainer. All these activities provided valuable insight into the previously unknown world of pre-school children and their families.

Building on this personal experience, the aim of my research was to give women returners an opportunity to talk about their career break experiences and the resulting professional development that *they* felt had taken place. As a deliberate attempt to validate that experience, it falls within the feminist research paradigm.

The Interview Programme

During the supply teachers' retraining course itself, members had an opportunity to write about their career break experiences. They were asked to reflect on what they thought they were bringing back into teaching as a direct result of their career break. This was done in an unstructured way: course members were merely asked to write freely in response to that request. I explained that my interest had been aroused by their comments at interview and that I wished to follow this up in more detail. Their written responses were to be anonymous. Towards the end of the course I explained that I had become so involved in this area that I wanted to follow up the previous feedback they had given by interviewing some in greater detail about their career break and return to the primary classroom.

This resulted in interviews in some depth with six women from the course. Whilst this is a small sample, it did constitute half the membership of that particular course. Each interview was conducted in the interviewee's own home. This was partly because in many cases it was easier for me to travel than it was for them, but also because experience of home visiting during my teaching career suggested that the women might feel more relaxed and less inhibited if they were in familiar surroundings and I was the invited guest.

The aim was to convey a general sense of returners' attitudes and experience, by distilling from detailed work with a small group. The written material and interview transcripts were analysed in some detail, seeking to identify common themes emerging from the data. After much deliberation, I concluded that the most powerful way of communicating the flavour of these themes would be to rely heavily on direct quotation to allow the women to speak for themselves. After presenting the major findings of my study, this chapter discusses some emerging issues.

Primary Themes

From analysis of all the data available, two major themes emerged. The first was that these women felt they had gained a much greater understanding of child development and individual differences. The second was that they acquired a deepening understanding of the parental perspective in education and thus a much deeper commitment to the notion of partnership in education. While other themes emerged which are discussed later, these two themes stood out as having a major impact on the thinking of these women.

Knowing Children as Individuals

First, the issue of child development and individual differences: it was very clear that these women felt that the experience of having children of their own and the time they spent at home with them had been significant in increasing their understanding of child development. This 'first-hand' knowledge was something that was constantly referred to and it was interesting to note how often this was contrasted with the more remote learning within their teacher training course:

> Although a lot of these things are taught within the college course they only fully come home with your own children.

> We did child development [at college] but it's terribly removed from the actual children.

> It's different actually . . . being told in *theory* and actually seeing it in practice.

One comment which appeared to summarize a general view was:

> Watching my own children develop was more informative than any amount of theory.

A common thread within this theme was that of knowing children 'as a whole'.

> I learnt that children are human, they're people, which I don't think I'd ever really thought before . . . and that they're all very different and have different thoughts and worries and interests . . . how individual everybody is.

> When I taught before I tended to lump them together . . . like the little vessels to be filled, I thought more of teaching them things . . . I hadn't thought of them as people.

The greater understanding of children as a whole also led to a greater appreciation of individual children's needs and difficulties. Experience of having their own children had made them more prepared to accept children as they were:

> You've got to just take them as they come and to allow them to progress at their own pace.

Some mentioned that they didn't really *know* any children before going into teaching.

> And, in fact, though I *liked* children before I went into teaching and thought I could *teach* them, I didn't *know* many children . . .

This view appeared to result in the view that when returning to teaching they would want to get to know children as individuals in greater depth:

> I'll make more effort to get to know them as an individual . . . rather than teaching them *en masse* as being a class.

Within this theme of getting to know children as individuals, two other sub-themes emerged. The first was the feeling that they would treat children's worries much more seriously than they had before. There was a feeling that they had been apt to dismiss many of the worries children expressed as being trivial, whereas their experience of motherhood had taught them to take these concerns more seriously. For example:

> All the sort of little problems that they have . . . sort of you know if they forget something . . . you know they're terribly terribly worried about that one thing . . . you know that they're really frightened that they've not brought their reading book . . . you realize that it's not the end of the world really . . . you get everything in perspective.

The second of these sub-themes was a growing awareness of the particular needs of quiet children. Those who felt they had largely ignored this group of children in the past hoped they would adopt a different attitude to them in the future. This was perhaps best summed up by the statement:

> I wouldn't be saying 'Thank goodness I've got those ten who are extremely quiet'. And, I mean I can remember thinking just that . . . aren't they wonderful these quiet children . . . they get on and do that and you just think they're problem-free because they're giving you no problems but . . . I'd *involve* them a lot more.

There was an admission that quiet children had been given a raw deal in the past:

> I hate this attitude that you give all the boisterous ones . . . parts in the school play and leave them [the quiet ones] out. My daughter's so quiet and yet she desperately wanted to be in things and one day after all the performances when she'd left the infants she said . . . 'You know, they *never* asked me'.

There appeared to be a tendency to more relaxed views on discipline, recognizing the need to get more involved in personal and social education, particularly with disruptive children, rather than merely tightening up on disciplinary measures.

Parental Perspectives

The second of the major themes emerging from analysis of the data relates to parents. A deeper understanding of the parental perspective was mentioned by every course member and was discussed in detail by those interviewed. There was, first, a recognition of the important role of parents in relation to the education and well-being of children. Course members felt they could now see things from the parents' point of view and were more tolerant of parents as a result. Some would be less intimidated by parents in the future while admitting to having been frightened of them in the past.

> I was always vaguely frightened of parents. They were always there to criticize me given a chance.

A feeling of having been insensitive in their dealings with parents in the past was also quite common. There was a strong sense that parents were a vital resource for the teacher in that they are the people closest to the child:

> I'll take more notice of what they say . . .

> I'll be taking more note of people who are actually closest to the child.

Building on the experience of concern about her own child's lack of progress at school, one woman declared:

> I'd listen to a mother who's saying that to me rather than fob her off. It's taken me nagging for two years for them to even recognize that she's falling behind.

This need to listen to parents reached across all backgrounds:

> I think that goes right the way across the backgrounds of children . . . to listen to what parents have to say . . . I think that mothers can often tell you a lot about why the child behaves so badly or whatever . . . and not just to write the child off but to find some way of understanding them.

Women mentioned the need for parental anxiety to be recognized and for teachers to be more reassuring, particularly if concern had already been expressed.

> The day you're worried about your child starting a new class and you've left them unhappy . . . if only they'd come out and say at the end of the day 'Jimmy's had a lovely day and he's been fine' . . . it doesn't take much . . . that's all a parent needs . . . and it makes them so much happier.

These former teachers confessed to having been irritated by parents in the past when they failed to do something that was expected of them. Their attitude had completely changed after experiencing at first-hand the pressures of family life.

> Well the mother that forgets to send the dinner money that I used to get totally exasperated with, but I can see quite well now how it happens . . .

One woman remembered during the earlier part of her career:

> feeling, you know, sort of disgust at parents when they didn't send the PE bag in on a Wednesday and they didn't have their names in their clothes and they'd forgotten their reading book . . . and they'd been too busy that night for Johnny to read his book and I used to think . . . well . . . you know . . . I was aghast at all this . . . you can't believe that these are so inadequate, these people.

She continued,

> I mean now I know what it's like trying to get a 5-year-old to school.

Certainly, there was evidence of a more sympathetic approach towards dinner-money problems since being involved themselves:

> Those little things . . . I got exasperated with the ones who didn't have the right money or the change . . . or . . . the one that sends a cheque every week . . . like me [laughs] . . .

A general thread running through comments was that they now had more understanding of what was involved in getting children to school each morning:

> The organization involved in getting children to school on time with the correct things they need for the day looking neat, clean and fed is not to be taken for granted.

'Parents' evenings' was an issue raised in several interviews, reflected in the comment that 'so many teachers are on the defensive . . . they feel criticized'. There was a feeling that they hoped they would be able to handle criticism more constructively in the future.

> I'm hoping that I can take it and not feel criticized . . . take it on board and build on it.

One reaction to their experience of parents' evenings was the sense that what *they*, as parents, felt didn't really matter. Two women interviewed expressed a desire to get involved in home visiting in an attempt to reach out to parents.

> Home visiting is something I'd go for in a big way because you can get so much out of visiting a parent in their own home rather than them being all still and tense.

Playtime and the Wider World
There was a changed attitude to playtime and its accompanying problems, and it was clear that this had not been an area where they had felt involved in the past. This matches my own view of playtime as a significant area of school life largely ignored by teachers, researchers and more especially HMI in school inspections (Green, 1985). Being a parent had clearly forced them to look at playtime in a new light:

> You've no idea when you've not had children, all the little things about going out in the playground . . . it's just trivial to you as a teacher.

The need for more teacher intervention was strongly felt.

> There is a genuine nastiness between the little groups and I think in some ways you've got to do something about it . . .
>
> It can be horrible for one or two children . . .
>
> I think really I'd be wanting to get involved.
>
> It gets to a dangerous level when they don't want to come to school because of a particular child.
>
> You know the little fall outs they have . . . you know you just say 'go away it'll be all right' but some things do need the teacher to intervene and you know . . . all the little heartaches they have and you as a parent feel them dreadfully and you say 'Go on, go off and be brave . . . cope' and the teacher really often has no idea.

A deeper understanding was mentioned of the wider range of influences on children — brothers and sisters, peer groups, television, parental expectations — and they were now more able to put the child's school experience into a wider context. Experience with younger children had led to a much greater understanding of the powerfully educative role of play in the child's life. Exposure to children's books and toys in the intimate setting of the home was also considered valuable in terms of professional development.

Professional Growth
Going into their child's school as a voluntary helper during the career break was found to be a valuable source of professional development — a rare opportunity to see other teachers at work.

> Going into school as a parent helper for many years involved in a variety of activities has also proved very useful in appreciating different approaches and methods used by individual teachers even within the same school.

Experiences of various forms of voluntary work outside teaching were cited as valuable in terms of professional development, while just being *away* from schools had given them time to reflect on teaching.

> Observing my own children's education has made me more critical and made me look at why I am teaching ... and what I'm teaching ... Would I be satisfied with that for my children? ... I think my standards will rise.

A final theme was that of the personal qualities they felt they were bringing back into teaching as a result of their career break. The qualities most commonly mentioned were maturity, patience and tolerance towards children and parents:

> ... *tolerance* of ... of children and their little whims ... and of parents and particularly mothers and their sort of ... problems.

What shines through all the evidence is that the women returners who were the focus of this research viewed their career break in very positive terms. They all felt that they had learned a great deal during this period which was of direct professional relevance to their future teaching. Undoubtedly the experience had resulted in a major shift in their attitudes, especially in two key areas — understanding children's individual needs and understanding the parental perspective in education.

Training and Appointment Issues

There is such strong evidence of professional growth during this period that the career break could well be regarded as a major component of these returners' in-service education. This, of course, currently comes absolutely free of charge to the employer. Whilst some teachers can get full-paid secondment to go into industry in order to bring their new insights back into the classroom, no one has yet suggested that women be given secondment to experience child-rearing at first-hand. Why, we may ask, should the very idea sound slightly preposterous whereas there is a general acceptance (albeit not in all circles) that secondment to industry is a reasonable way to spend public funds? In fact, as a lecturer in higher education, I recently received funding from the Department of Trade and Industry in order to gain experience of the 'world of work' and spent, as a result, a largely fruitless day watching someone fail to sell insurance policies to various members of the public. I have considerable doubts about the value of such experiences in terms of professional development, yet such schemes sometimes seem to be subjected to little scrutiny in terms of their professional relevance.

Kath Green

The evidence of this research is that the women themselves regard their career break as a major part of their professional development. At the very least, the government, LEAs and governing bodies should recognize this by seeing that one year's experience counts as one incremental point on the salary scale. Sadly, I say this at a time when there is an unprecedented threat to the placing of any value at all on these forms of experience.

The new funding arrangements for schools threaten to devalue career break experience. LEAs, who over the years have developed salary policies which at least gave some recognition to the value of career break experiences, are in a position where they no longer insist that these policies are adhered to. If governing bodies choose to ignore these experiences totally when assessing both starting and re-entry salaries, then LEAs are powerless to act.

Regular contact with returners, headteachers and mature students indicates that 'flexibility' in staffing policies is resulting in discrimination against returners. Some heads have made it clear that experience is now seen as a negative factor in appointments because of the increasingly tight budgets that schools have to manage. I am currently engaged in a joint project with colleagues in two other ITT institutions in order to research this area. Some returners are pre-empting the issue by declaring at an early stage in the appointing process that they are willing to be considered for appointment below the salary level to which they ought to be entitled. This is an appalling indictment of present government policy.

The career break of women teachers should be valued in not just monetary terms but also in terms of the wider experience which these teachers bring back to the classroom. In job applications the career break is an area largely ignored both on application forms and at interviews. There are two ways of putting this on the agenda for interviews.

The first would involve training for governors, headteachers and local authority advisers and officers so that they realize that this is an important part of women returners' professional development and, therefore, a legitimate subject for discussion at interview. The second step would be to see that women play a larger part in the interviewing process so that the all-male interviewing panel becomes a thing of the past. A possible danger in some current equal opportunities developments with regard to good practice in interviewing is that discussion of an important part of many women's lives could be ruled 'out of bounds'. Whilst happy to ban questions on family planning or child-minding arrangements, I don't think the interests of women are properly served by banning *all* questions relating to aspects of their lives outside the 'normal' career path.

So far this chapter has identified issues and their implications, validating my previous views on the subject (though nonetheless valid for that). In terms of my personal learning two other themes emerge from this research relevant to interview methods and to teacher training.

Issues for Researchers

The first has been the powerful way in which engaging in this research process has highlighted issues of methodology in ways which no theoretical reading of the literature could have done. Each interview was part of a learning process for both myself and the interviewee. Helen Simons refers to this when she claims that interviews 'can be an educational process as interviewees begin to reflect on their own situation and perhaps continue the inquiry beyond the formal interviews' (Simons, 1981, p. 33). This was certainly true on those occasions where the interviewees were still raising issues and thinking further while on the doorstep to wave farewell. One interviewee said 'I'm bound to think of lots more things as soon as you've gone', making it clear that she would go on thinking about the issues that had been discussed after my departure. Finally, she took a note of my address so that she could write with further comments when she had more time to think it through. Further than that, I believe each interview was also educational for me in encouraging further reflection on many issues and gave new insights on my own career break.

In terms of the interviewees' experience of the interview, there was positive comment on each occasion that they had enjoyed the experience. This again matches Finch's experience (1984) who argued that this was due to the special nature of women interviewing women. She argued that women were used to being asked questions about their lives by an assortment of professionals, that the home setting made it more intimate and that women's structural position in the domestic sphere meant that they would welcome opportunities to talk.

Finch argued that the special character of women interviewing women is as much political as methodological. However good the male interviewer, there will be an added dimension when the interviewer is a woman in that 'both parties share a subordinate structural position by virtue of their gender' (Finch, 1984, p. 76). Certainly these women were very willing to talk about key areas of their lives in ways which showed a high level of trust and which indicated that they thought

I would understand what they meant because I was a woman. Indeed, I would agree that 'the ease with which one can get women to talk in the interview situation depends not so much upon one's skills as an interviewer, nor upon one's expertise as a sociologist, but upon one's identity as a woman' (Finch, 1984).

One particular interviewee became somewhat defensive and uncomfortable when talking about the number of years she had spent at home with young children. However, as soon as she discovered that I had had a similar length of career break she immediately began talking much more positively about the experience. I sensed at the time that she may have felt threatened by the possibility that I had not shared this experience and might even disapprove of the length of her career break. Interestingly, Finch (1984) found some unease when an interviewee was in doubt as to how to place her in relation to categories of marriage and motherhood. This need to 'place' the interviewer has also been reported by Oakley (1981).

This issue of motive and commitment lies at the heart of much feminist research. I can well remember my surprise on meeting a group of educational researchers who were clearly not remotely interested in talking about their previous research. They were apparently not really involved in the subject area or committed to the research; it had merely been seen as a means of 'getting on'.

The easily established trust which can build up in the interview situation can make women vulnerable to exploitation, and puts a heavy responsibility on the interviewer. The researcher needs to anticipate whether others may use the research in ways not intended by the original researcher (Platt, 1984; Roberts, 1981). This could also be true of my research where, while wanting to value women's role at home during their career break, I would not want to provide ammunition for those who would wish to force all women with children to stay at home. (e.g., John Selwyn Gummer, 'Panorama', BBC 18 September 1989)

Finch resolved the dilemma by making a clear distinction between the structured position in which the women were placed and their personal experience of it, thus enabling her to see 'that evidence of women successfully accommodating to various structured features of their lives in no way alters the essentially exploitative character of the structures in which they are located' (Finch, 1984, p. 84). She believes the dilemmas are moral ones which are also political in character: 'They raise the "whose side are we on?" question in a particular form.'

It has been common in research ethics to distinguish between research on powerless social groups and on the powerful. The feminist stance of being on the side of the women we study is consistent with traditional sociological research where the sociologist sides with 'the underdog' (Becker, 1967; Barnes, 1979). 'One essential difference, however, is that a feminist sociologist doing research on women actually shares the powerless position of those she researches' (Finch, 1984) — a situation not often paralleled by men unless perhaps they are black sociologists working on race.

Being on the side of those we research involves emotional commitment and endorses Oakley's (1981) position that as a feminist and sociologist one should be creating a sociology *for* women. She sees the changing role of the interview from that of 'a data collecting instrument for researchers to being a data collecting instrument for those whose lives are being researched' (Oakley, 1981, p. 49).

Issues for Teacher Educators

The other theme from this research has emerged more slowly towards the end of the research process as I began to stand back and reflect on some of the issues arising. This theme concerns the implications for teacher education. All the women interviewed felt that the experience of bringing up children had been a major focus for their learning in the area of child development. Their sustained involvement with individual children provided a vehicle for much learning about child development and individual differences. They all felt they would alter their future teaching as a result.

As teacher educators we need to think again about how we could try to get the 'individual child perspective' more clearly incorporated into our ways of teaching student teachers. We need to base our courses more firmly in the experiential mould of helping students first of all to get to know individual children and to begin to understand their personal worlds. Above all, students need time to work with very small groups of children so that they do not lose sight of the children as individuals in their attempts to control them as a class.

This does, of course, run completely counter to a dominant current trend, which is the view of young children as 'vessels to be filled'. In my own career, the experience of fostering a 'special needs' child and watching him go through the education system was a growth point in my own professional development. When asked to lead 'special needs' sessions, I have often simply told his story in very personal terms knowing that it will be a powerful way of teaching about children with special needs. Above all then, it is the *valuing of personal experience*, whether that of individual children or of the women supply teachers who were the subject of this study, which has perhaps become the major implication of my work. As Ann Oakley so clearly recognized:

> personal involvement is more than dangerous bias — it is the condition under which people come to know each other and to admit others into their lives. (Oakley, 1981, p. 58)

References

BARNES, J. (1979) *Who Should Know What?*, Harmondsworth, Penguin.
BECKER, H. (1967) 'Whose Side Are We On' in BELL, C. and ROBERTS, H. (Eds) (1984) *Social Researching: Politics, Problems, Practice*, London, Routledge and Kegan Paul.
FINCH, J. (1984) 'It's great to have someone to talk to: the ethics and politics of interviewing women', in BELL, C. and ROBERTS, H. (Eds) (1984) *Social Researching: Politics, Problems, Practices*, London, Routledge and Kegan Paul.
GREEN, K. (1985) *Out to Play*, in *The Times Educational Supplement*, 21 October.
OAKLEY, A. (1981) 'Interviewing Women: a contradiction in terms' in ROBERTS, H. (Ed.) *Doing Feminist Research*, London, Routledge and Kegan Paul.
PLATT, J. (1984) 'The Affluent Worker Re-visited' in BELL, C. and ROBERTS, H. (Eds) *Social Researching: Politics, Problems, Practice*, London, Routledge and Kegan Paul.
ROBERTS, H. (Ed.) (1981) *Doing Feminist Research*, London, Routledge and Kegan Paul.
SIMONS, H. (1981) 'Conversation Piece: the practice of interviewing in case study research', in ADELMAN, C. (Ed.) (1981) *Uttering, Muttering: Collecting, Using and Reporting Talk for Social and Educational Research*, London, Grant Mcintyre.

Chapter 3

Highlighting a Grey Area

Mary Mullett

This chapter describes the formation and evolution of the Milton Keynes Supply Teachers' Support Group. With five original members, the author highlights what is possible when a group of enthusiastic professionals draw on formal and informal contacts to establish much needed support and resourcing for a local initiative. The narrative also illustrates the role of intervening agencies in influencing the direction of development, in this case towards returners' schemes. With further changes in school-LEA relations and most founder members now back in full-time teaching posts, conclusions refocus our attention on the contribution of key agents in educational change. Here the author's sustained drive and enthusiasm leads to an acceleration of efforts to seek a national focus of interest in an area currently awaiting a sense of political immediacy among those who govern.

The Origins and Growth of the Support Group

Beginnings are often fuzzy and blurred but there was a beginning and there were five of us: Joan, Edwina, Yvonne, Jackie and me, Mary. We used to meet in the primary school playground most mornings and afternoons, taking and collecting young children from school. Some of us knew each other already from our children's nursery class days. We had discovered that we were ex-teachers and wondered when, if at all, we might teach again. We had enjoyed the time at home but as our children settled into playgroup or school we felt the need to teach again.

One by one we began to start supply work and talked over experiences. Looking back I realize that we all cared very much about doing a good job. Some days the work went well. But on other occasions we felt frustrated and disappointed. Had we lost our teaching skills? How could they be regained? Then we realized that the nature of supply work itself seemed to prevent us feeling satisfied with what we achieved with the children. We agreed that the job could make us feel rather lonely and isolated. We decided to meet, on a professional basis, to see if we could help each other.

So, on a snowy evening 1 January 1985 we gathered at my home in Wolverton. It was the first meeting of what became the Milton Keynes 'Supply Teachers' Support Group' which met, off and on, for five years. I still remember the feeling of relief as we shared experiences that night about teaching the previous term. Soon there were gales of laughter as we saw the amusing side of situations which had previously, in private, not felt funny at all. Over the next few weeks we shared thoughts about useful books, games and activities for 'one-off' days of supply work when the schools asked us to bring in suitable work. But often the part of the evening we enjoyed and valued most was to talk through the experience of teaching itself. This was something which we remembered when we later came to plan support group meetings for numbers of fifteen or more. We always started with refreshments to allow time for talk and built in time before the meeting finished for more informal exchange of ideas. To this day when a KIT meeting reaches a half-time break I relish the buzz of conversation which invariably starts up. (KIT stands for 'Keep in Touch with Teaching.)

We realized back then in 1985 that our teaching experiences were improving and sometimes it was simply that we had more confidence and this communicated itself to the children and to our full-time colleagues in school. At one early meeting we discussed how to settle quickly into an unfamiliar school. I was working in secondary schools, large organizations on big sites. It was sometimes hard, in a school new to me, to gather the information needed, such as map, lesson times, wet-break arrangements, and so on. Yet without that information my credibility with pupils immediately became suspect. Amused tolerance would be the best one could hope for. 'With-itness' was essential for successful supply teaching just as it had been for full-time teaching.

The other four founder members were working in primary and special schools; they too needed basic information on arrival at a new school. From that session came the idea of a 'check-list' of information for visiting supply teachers. One founder member was married to a primary headteacher. Two had partners working full-time in primary schools. We therefore had access to perspectives on what schools thought of supply teachers, not always a comfortable assessment. Equally the partners now saw at home the hard work that went into preparing for supply teaching and began to wonder how schools could enhance the support that many did already offer to supply staff. The 'check-list', one for primary, one for secondary, was drawn up on one side of A4 for schools to complete. This included (for primary) name of headteacher, secretary, session times, register and dinner-time procedures, whereabouts of stationery, wet-break arrangements, any special fire-drill instructions, reading and maths schemes used and so on.

With the intention of sharing ideas with other supply teachers in our area, two of the group saw the area education officer and explained our idea for the check-list and for widening the membership of the group. We explained that this was not a pressure group but hoped to meet, on a professional basis, for the mutual benefit of supply teachers and the schools with whom they worked. He suggested that the senior support teacher (then Beryl Marriott) became our link with the office, and he offered to have our check-lists typed up and introduced at a headteachers' meeting. All eighty-eight (then) schools in Milton Keynes responded and soon there was a completed check-list in each school office, available for supply teachers to see on arrival.

From time to time the Area office sent a circular to all supply teachers so a brief notice about the support group was included with the next circular, announcing an evening meeting. From a total of over 180 supply teachers sixty expressed an interest and forty attended that first general meeting in May 1985, at the Queensway Centre in Bletchley. They completed information slips which invited them to say which topics they would like to see covered in future meetings. We also asked if anyone would be willing to host a meeting in their own town for a local group, as travel to Bletchley was difficult and time-consuming for many members. One satellite group formed in Stony Stratford.

As we grew in confidence we invited County advisers and staff in schools to speak and also discovered that once members had had a chance to talk through their personal concerns they wanted more substance in their meetings. The National Curriculum was beginning to arrive in schools and supply teachers needed help to understand it so that they could work effectively with children and full-time colleagues.

After consulting with members, I used my links with the office, secondary contacts met in the course of my own supply teaching, and primary contacts offered through the primary membership, to establish topics and speakers for meetings. This could be quite time-consuming but I enjoyed it and learnt a lot on the way. I wrote a short letter from my home address about once a term with details of planned meetings, dates and speakers.

The education office typed these and posted them to all supply teachers in Milton Keynes, so covering the cost of the letter distribution and the labour involved. Later, as the workload in the office began to grow with the impact of the Education Acts, I went into the office to help. I checked supply teacher lists and put letters into envelopes, ensuring no duplications, as we realized anew that some people were on primary, secondary and special school lists. Speakers at Support Group meetings generously gave their time: I contributed to our burgeoning family phone bill from my supply pay.

In common with some other authorities, Buckinghamshire did not then make a hiring charge to a genuine education group meeting; this was another fundamental factor in enabling the voluntary group to flourish. Word spread and we began to see those 'thinking about starting supply teaching' at meetings and realized the group was addressing the teacher retention factor too.

In June 1986 there was some correspondence in the *Times Educational Supplement* (20 June 1986) about supply teacher shortages and issues about status and working conditions. I contributed a positive letter about the support group. In the same year (with the agreement of the office), my article for '*Child Education*' (Mullett, 1986) about the group stimulated several letters from other LEAs and from individual supply teachers who had local networks or wanted to establish one. In 1988 we were visited by the *Times Educational Supplement* and this article (24 June 1988) produced further contact from outside the county. Other LEAs were interested in the way the group functioned, individual schools wanted copies of the check-list and supply teachers wrote in modest numbers from all over the country to ask for tips on how to set up a group in their area. The issues for supply teachers seemed similar wherever they might be living.

During 1988 the group also decided to draw together the shared experiences and expertise in a guide on primary supply teaching for colleagues in Milton Keynes (Johnson and Mullett, 1988). Yvonne and I wrote most of this together, with very helpful contributions and comments from Edwina, Joan and others. Again the office supported us with input from Barrie Brown (senior support teacher) and Andrew Flack, educational officer. The guide was printed by Buckinghamshire County Council and Yvonne and I introduced it at a Milton Keynes primary headteachers' meeting and gave each school a copy. I was surprised to see how many heads I recognized and of course Yvonne had worked in several of the schools. We were warmly received.

As the months and years went by the original five members moved on, some to part-time and then full-time work. Two of us continued to find supply teaching the most appropriate form of service for us. I valued very much the contact I maintained with colleagues through the changing membership of the group and learnt much about their concerns and priorities in the meetings.

The Research into Supply Teacher Issues

The support group has been described in some detail because it was important and the information also provides a context for what follows. In the spring of 1989 Buckinghamshire, together with other County Councils, was celebrating its centenary, with functions in each area. Two of us were invited to the Milton Keynes event to represent local supply teachers.

At the same period there was an acute shortage of primary supply teachers in Milton Keynes in the Spring term. More would be needed to work in first schools with the rising fives in the summer term. National Curriculum training was taking staff out of every school and the expansion of schools as part of the Milton Keynes Development plan also filtered down to require more teachers and hence more occasional supply cover.

At the county reception I was introduced to the chief education officer, who knew of the group and asked what I thought would encourage supply teachers to work more frequently. He asked me to put my ideas in writing and an invitation to the Milton Keynes area office followed to work on a special project about primary supply teaching (Mullett, 1989a) involving Linda Rougale (assistant area education officer), Barrie Brown and others. It was Linda's idea to draw up a questionnaire for primary supply teachers to gather some statistics about supply teachers. The paper I had written for the CEO was one starting point for formulating the survey (See Appendix 1). Officers' ideas were included to cover additional issues on which the authority needed clarification.

It was hoped that the results of the survey would inform policy making. I was invited to undertake the research and to extend it to the other three areas in Buckinghamshire: Aylesbury Vale, Wycombe and Chiltern/South Bucks. Enthusiastic about the project, I looked forward to visiting new areas of the county, with the following brief:

> The research will be designed to find out how we can improve supply teacher provision, what supply teachers feel are their

needs and preferences, and what professional obligations we can expect from our supply teachers. (LEA officer's letter to the author, April 1989)

Initially I had 100 hours (extended eventually to 177.5 hours) for a number of tasks:

- to visit the other areas to be aware of their local issues;
- compose the pilot survey and distribute it to agreed people;
- make amendments in the light of their comments;
- despatch main survey and process results;
- write commentary on results;
- draw conclusions and make recommendations; and
- write up the whole document.

The Milton Keynes area office would provide administrative support, stationery, postage and so on and I was to be paid on my normal supply rates. After visiting other areas I started to write the questionnaire. Joan's husband, a senior lecturer at the Open University, helped clarify the internal structure of the questionnaire and lent background reading.

Linda suggested revisions to the questions and explanatory comments which introduced each of the six sections of the survey and helped me to write in the 'house style'. The County IT adviser agreed to write the software to help process the results. He worked on the pilot survey and the final version and offered a perspective as a county-wide adviser.

The pilot survey was distributed to a small cross-section of the support group membership and also to some supply teachers who had not come to support group meetings and who therefore came fresh to the issues raised. Response to the first posting of the survey and covering letter was slow which was a problem because the time to process and write the report had been reduced since the planning of the questionnaire. A further letter of encouragement produced additional responses and the processing and analysis was able to start. The final response rate was 46 per cent of the circulation.

I read all the returns and coded them; the information was processed and problems checked with me. Another office assistant noted and collated the open-ended answers and I read and reported on them. The IT adviser helped to elicit further statistics and cross-referenced information.

Highlighting a Grey Area

I finished work on 24 June which enabled the report to be printed before the end of term and of the academic year. Those who had given so much time to the project on top of their daily workload were keen to see it be read and used.

After the Research

I spent a quiet summer holiday thinking occasionally about the Autumn term's support group programme, privileged to have learnt a great deal more from the research about the needs and aspirations of supply teacher colleagues. In October that year I contacted County Hall to see if there were any further developments on supply issues and was invited to Aylesbury to meet the Deputy CEO, Dr Keith Robinson, and Ivan Andrew, area education officer for Aylesbury Vale.

Keith told me that the report had been circulated internally in the Education Department and the feeling was that it would be helpful if a report on the research was prepared for all headteachers in Bucks, including secondary and special schools. Would I like to do it? This unexpected invitation involved a base in the Aylesbury Vale area office and Ivan would give support and introductions to the secondary and special-school headteachers. Some work on supply teacher issues in those fields of education would obviously be needed. I felt confident about embarking on that because I had been doing supply teaching in a variety of secondary and special school contexts (and reflecting on the issues) for six years.

The Report for Headteachers in Buckinghamshire

The Autumn term and into January 1990 were devoted to this new report which, besides providing the conclusions and recommendations of the earlier research, was to include an appropriate presentation of further selected details of the results of the survey. Visits were made to five secondary schools, including a grammar school and an upper school to meet either the headteacher or the deputy with responsibility for supply teacher provision. I also liaised with several special schools.

On these visits I used notes on what the issues might be for recruiting and retaining effective secondary supply staff and sounded out schools on their views and strategies. There was general agreement that the non-professional reasons for doing supply teaching might be almost identical to the primary teachers' reasons. This was certainly my experience but only further research could test this hypothesis.

Mary Mullett

The report for headteachers (Mullett, 1990) explained the reasons for the original research, and why the results were felt to be of use to the whole county. The research was summarized, particularly in the areas of classroom practice and how schools work with supply teachers. A new section discussed primary supply teachers and the National Curriculum. The section on secondary supply teacher issues offered a definition of an effective secondary supply teacher, and considered induction, continuity for supply staff and pupils, changes in supply personnel, and cover for extended absence. A further note applied to headteachers of special schools.

The conclusions and recommendations adopted a different emphasis and tone from the original study, and included items on retention, recruitment and communication. The appendix was followed by a form for feedback on the report.

Presenting the New Report to Headteachers in Aylesbury Vale

At Central Printing I took some pleasure in choosing a grey front cover with a bright-red spiral binding. Knowing how much paperwork was arriving in schools at the time I hoped heads would actually feel like reading the report. Ivan had taken an active interest in the work and suggested that it be introduced at one of his meetings with Aylesbury Vale primary heads and I was pleased to do this. On the day, in a school hall full of headteachers, I held aloft the grey cover with the distinctive red binding and nothing between the covers because the meeting date, fixed months before, had come before the reports had been printed. This raised a laugh and I explained that these colours had been chosen so that the red spine would 'highlight a grey area', which defined how I felt about supply teaching. The hope was that they would remember the cover when they saw it in their post at school.

Developments Since the Research

Towards the end of the next term (Summer 1990) Linda Rougale asked me with others to meet some teachers who were thinking of returning to teaching. The idea was to have a meeting with them before the end of term and then work towards providing an updating course for primary returners in the following term. Not all those who responded to

Highlighting a Grey Area

the local newspaper advertisement were able to come to the meeting but they were assured that their names would be kept on file at the office to be sent details of the course. Some support group members present were thinking of applying for part-time/full-time posts. Later that term I was asked to work on a part-time, temporary basis for two terms to set up a KITS scheme for Milton Keynes. KITS stood for 'Keeping In touch with Teaching and Supply teacher support'. The 'S' part of the title was important. The brief was to set up a register of teachers in a career break, write a newsletter for them and the supply teachers, run appropriate meetings, be involved with planning the forthcoming course and be available for people to come and see me — Linda would be my line manager. I was really pleased to be involved: the needs of support-group members would be met by this arrangement which gave the original group members enormous satisfaction.

During those two terms with Linda's help I began to understand the slightly different emphasis and support needed for teachers still in the middle of their career break and learnt more about educational administration and how to prepare copy for the printers and so on. Most of all I enjoyed welcoming and getting to know returning colleagues and seeing them grow in confidence. A highlight was the first evening of the supply teachers' training course, something we had hoped for for so long.

The scheme was well received and followed by an invitation to coordinate a County-wide KIT scheme from April 1991 on a one year, part-time basis, working with each of the four areas in partnership. Initially the responsibility was for a county KIT newsletter and organizing two meetings per term in each area as well as keeping a file of KIT membership forms and being an initial point of contact and referral for enquirers. I had thirty days a term to deliver the scheme and met many more members and headteachers throughout the county. Later a twice-termly system of individual appointments was set up in each of the four areas so that people could come on a one-to-one basis to discuss their particular concerns. The scheme took off well, and my contract was renewed in April 1992 for one year.

I relished the opportunity to try out new ideas for meetings which area offices and the membership had suggested. The newsletters were circulated to all the schools and sometimes headteachers would phone to see if there were members who might be interested in applying for an unexpected vacancy. Returners could of course be available for posts after the deadline for giving notice had expired for full-time colleagues, and a number of KIT members were successful at interview, against competition, and were launched back into teaching.

I now understood more about the financial background to education, from working in County Hall on the newsletter, liaising with advisers, officers and the areas to making sure newsletter articles were accurate and relevant. So I saw at second-hand the impact of new legislation as the department worked hard to implement it. The school where I am a governor had been a pilot school for LFM then LMS and I had attended governor training relating to the legislation. So when it was announced, in late autumn 1992, that the GEST funding would end for recruitment and retention initiatives in April 1993 I understood that my post could not be funded further. My disappointment was tempered by an increased awareness of education issues within a much wider financial context which helped in coming to terms with the decision.

More importantly the 1666 teachers who received the KIT newsletter would miss the support of the full scheme, though the areas and my current line manager were committed to its worth and planning what could be offered in the future. So in the time that remained in post I wrote a KIT handbook for career break teachers in Buckinghamshire to draw together articles from the six county newsletters and add new material and advice to suit the current situation (Mullett, 1993). It was also, hopefully, a useful document to offer to new enquirers about KIT.

The Future

At time of writing it is still a changing world in education, and this filters down to my supply teaching contacts too. They find that work is no longer available in the same way as before LMS. Supply teachers who taught for eight or nine years before their career break are concerned that they are expensive, even unemployable. Those who need to earn money but cannot offer full-time work hope that job-share may become more available and attractive to schools. As more specialized subject knowledge is needed to deliver the National Curriculum they wonder if a partnership offering different subject strengths might be welcomed.

Colleagues who have been involved with KIT schemes in other parts of the country know that in a few years' time there will be teacher shortages again and we will need to look to returners once more to fill the gap. It can take two or three years for a returner to be updated and feel confident and realistic about applying for a full-time post in school. So I am trying to see if interested bodies will plan

Highlighting a Grey Area

with me for a national KIT scheme which would encourage career-break teachers (including supply teachers) to continue to feel supported and valued and ready in due course to return to teaching. It is tempting to end with that tired old saying 'Watch this space!' By the time this is printed something relevant may be happening. In the meantime, to end where we began, here is news of the founding members of the support group, eight years later[1]:

> Joan Hammersley is now a senior teacher in a special school for children with moderate learning difficulties. She has responsibility for non-teaching staff, assessment, record keeping, English, lower school, primary parents and is the class teacher for the Reception/Year 1 class.
>
> Edwina Starkie is teaching full-time in a first school and was for eighteen months acting deputy head but has happily returned to senior management with responsibility for maths and a year group.
>
> Yvonne Johnson, who gave so much extra time to the group in the early days, is now teaching full-time in a combined primary school.
>
> Jackie Cobham is now teaching full-time in a first school and is the coordinator for science.
>
> Mary Mullett . . . well, you know what happened to me.

Note

1 None of my work with supply teachers and subsequently with career-break teachers would have been possible without their commitment or the support of schools and Buckinghamshire County Council's Education Department. I thank them all and stress that the views expressed in this chapter are my own.

References

JOHNSON, Y. and MULLETT, M. (1988) 'Guide for Primary Supply Teachers', Milton Keynes Supply Teachers' Support Group, Buckinghamshire County Council, October.

MULLETT, M. (1986) 'Supply and demand', in *Child Education*, October.
MULLETT, M. (1989) 'Research into primary supply teacher issues: results and report', Buckinghamshire County Council, Aylesbury Education Department, July.
MULLETT, M. (1990) 'Research into supply teacher issues: results and report for headteachers', Buckinghamshire County Council Education Department, Aylesbury, January.
MULLETT, M. (1993) 'Keeping in Touch with Teaching: A Handbook for Buckinghamshire Teachers in a Career Break', Buckinghamshire County Council Education Department, April.

Chapter 4

Temps in the Classroom: A Case of Hidden Identities?

Marlene Morrison

In the previous chapter, a story of the birth and evolution of a support network for supply teachers indicates what is possible when a sharing of experience is used to enhance and affirm professional skills. Turning to the chalk-face, this chapter explores professional identities and images of supply work as understood by permanent and temporary teachers, and experienced by the latter. In contexts of ambiguous and sometimes contradictory expectations, the author investigates complex perceptions underpinning strategies needed to keep a class 'ticking over' and offers challenging counterpoints to assumptions about teacher identities, which, until recently, have been largely dominated by permanent and full-time practitioners.

In our society work, and specifically paid employment, has become a prime claimant on individuals' lives. As Everett Hughes pointed out more than forty years ago, work is one of the ways we judge ourselves and are judged by others, an important aspect of 'social identity' and 'the self' (Hughes, 1951). In recent years, educational studies have focused increasingly on teachers' work. Among the approaches taken are analyses of the subjective experiences of teaching (Sikes, Measor, and Woods, 1985; Nias, 1988). Informed by symbolic interactionism, research has explored teacher identities and the development of professional and personal self-image. Nias, for example, has looked at the ways in which primary teachers' work 'calls for a massive investment of . . . "selves"' (Nias, 1989, p. 2); Woods' emphasis is on creative teachers whose activities are 'tempered' by constraints described on a continuum from 'golden opportunity' to 'leaden constraint' (Woods, 1990, p. 22).

Despite this growing emphasis on teachers' work, research into teachers and supply teaching remains sparse (Shilling, 1991; Galloway,

Marlene Morrison

1993). With the exception of a few specific studies (for example, Loveys, 1988; Trotter and Wragg, 1990), supply work has been considered primarily in relation to concerns about teacher absence (Brown and Earley, 1990) rather than its contribution to teaching and learning (Morrison, 1991; Morrison, 1993, and this volume). Substitute teachers are viewed with an ambivalence which acknowledges the need for them to be 'first rate teachers' (Shilling, 1991, p. 5) yet who 'are not full members of a school organisation and cannot realistically be expected to be treated as such' (op. cit., p. 4).

This chapter pursues a 'Hughesian directive' (Salaman, 1975, p. 159) to investigate personal and professional images of supply work which have remained largely invisible or assumed. It uses documentary evidence, interviews, and observation to explore the ways in which work is understood and experienced by supply teachers and permanent colleagues in primary school settings.

Research Contexts

Explorations focus on aspects of data collected by the author during 1991–2[1]. Detailed studies of supply teaching took place in two LEAs. Data used in this chapter refers to an authority called Centrelink, a metropolitan LEA selected to reflect an inner-city, multi-ethnic situation, and a specific approach to supply issues. In recent years Centrelink had experienced changes in its commercial and industrial infrastructure, and this was reflected partly in urban redevelopment programmes, a shift in population, and falling school rolls. Centrelink operated a primary supply/relief team cover scheme. In 1991–2 schools without delegated budgets had been expected to participate in the scheme. During that period, of the twenty-seven schools with the opportunity to opt out of the scheme, nine chose to do so. The establishment figure for the supply team was forty-two. Together with a centrally maintained casual supply register, these serviced the supply needs of an LEA which had ninety-eight primary schools.

Traditionally the LEA had fostered close links with schools. Programmes of in-service training and professional development took place at an education centre, where the primary supply team was also based. Throughout the investigation, financial, political, and educational changes posed significant challenges. With policy and practice at the LEA/school interface in transition, the future of the supply team was part of that uncertainty. In the accounts which follow, pseudonyms are used throughout.

The Self: Identities and Fleeting Relationships

Central to the concerns of this chapter are complex and multiple interpretations about what it means to work in temporally constrained educational settings. Because most commentaries on teacher identities assume a permanent work-force and regular relationships, few provide useful starting points for exploring understandings about supply teaching experience. Nias (1989) draws on previous work about the 'self' (Cooley, 1983 ed.; Mead, 1934) to explore teacher identities. Symbolic interactionists argue that 'through interaction with people to whose behaviour we attach symbolic meanings we learn to take other people's perspectives and so to see ourselves as we think they see us' (Nias, 1989, p. 19). From this perspective, 'significant others' have a powerful effect on identity (Cooley, 1983 ed., p. 175) as, through time, individuals internalize the attitudes of organized social groups — 'the generalised other' — (Mead, 1934). Nias points out that earlier writers like Ball (1972) have stressed the importance of an inner core — the 'substantial' self — which is resistant to such influences. In relation to primary teaching, Nias argues that whilst the 'substantial self' is not, by definition, an ephemeral phenomenon, the nature of teaching makes it difficult for individuals to remain immune from situational values' (Nias, 1989, p. 49). Moreover, because values are integral to the traditions, culture, and contexts of primary teaching, the latter 'makes heavy demands on the self' (op. cit., pp. 25–6). In the 'presentation of self to others', Goffman (1959) argues that in most interactions the tendency is for actors to move towards a kind of 'interactional *modus vivendi* . . . a working . . . veneer . . . of consensus' about 'the division of definitional labour' (pp. 30–1).

Unlike most permanent colleagues in primary schools, interactions between supply teachers and children, and between substitute and permanent teachers, are not infrequently ill-defined, and neither symmetrical nor regular. Instead, relationships are sometimes fleeting and transitory, and enacted in the presence of strangers (Morrison and Galloway, 1993). In different contexts, Davis (1965) notes that in more binding professional–client relationships, the 'modicum' of visible stability, continuity, and homogeneity, helps to prevent relationships becoming 'reputationless, anonymous, and narrowly calculative' (p. 336). Such a 'modicum' of 'constraints' is frequently absent from supply teacher relationships. Isolated from colleagues, and yet frequently exposed to values acquired in earlier teaching careers, supply teachers need to make sense of recurrent work problems in disparate situations. What are their self-images? To what extent do they identify with other teachers? What are the perceptions of 'significant others'? To what extent are these affected by, and reflected in, their experience of work situations? These were key issues for investigation. In important ways they connect with gendered images of supply teaching as 'women's work'.

Gender Stereotyping

Goffman's analysis (1959) throws further light on the stereotypes forged from fleeting or temporary interactions. Understandings by permanent teachers about temporary colleagues might be based on previous experiences of 'cover' teaching, or upon 'untested stereotypes' (p. 324). Throughout the research, the team focused on gender as a first-order construct which, on occasion, crystallized over perceptions about 'women's work' and terms like commitment, involvement, and confidence. Yet links between supply and women's work were frequently blurred and/or implicit, and ignored the contributions of male supply teachers. With discourse and anecdotes referring regularly to female images (the perhaps apocryphal negative image of the supply teacher who 'did her knitting' when 'covering' classes recurred in primary and secondary teacher interviews), gendered references were sometimes used to distinguish (and arguably distance) permanent teachers from temporary colleagues. In the following extract a supply team manager uses gender balance to contrast the team with those on the casual supply register. Referring to the latter she comments:

> They tend to be ladies. They've had a career break to have families and so they've used it to come back and test the water. Really, to get their confidence back because I think, a lot of them said to me that they had lost their confidence whilst being at home. Now some of the people that came back have had a year with us and have gone on. They feel, right, now I know what it's like, they want something to get their teeth into, supply teaching isn't for them all. Some want a permanent placement.

In other contexts, gender characteristics were sometimes used to reflect on possible links between supply teaching and effects on children's learning. A primary class teacher was asked to recall a specific example:

> I remember a man . . . who was one of the world's incompetents . . . they occur everywhere, nice gentle teachers who can't cope, men, they're often men, nice man he was . . . As soon as he walked through the door . . . the children ran him ragged. We managed to get him through a couple of days but he found it very hellish but I don't think they [the children] learnt anything . . . At least he got out of it alive. Well they did learn something, that they can run a teacher ragged.

However, more typical were comments about 'types' felt to be suited to supply work. In the following extract, an interviewee describes:

> People who have been on the team for years and years and like it. They came because they wanted experience but the Gipsy gets into them. It suits certain personality types I think, . . . Some people say 'Oh! I couldn't stand supply' . . . Some people actually like the uncertainty of getting through the morning and not knowing what class they'll have till they get there. I mean, other people, it fills them with horror, but some people actually thrive on that.

Such introductory themes are now explored more fully.

Teachers' Views

During the research, the two main reasons for teacher substitution were to cover teacher absence for illness and for in-service training. In recent years many aspects of each had altered. Interview data drew attention to teachers' perceptions that there was more of both kinds of absence. Not only had recent legislation required in-service training on a scale and of a kind that did not exist earlier, but interviews with heads, teachers and pupils were also peppered with references to absence through illness, directly or indirectly linked to teacher stress. Underlying the discussions was a kind of 'positioning' not untypical of 'the discursive production' of selves and others in conversation (Davies and Harré, 1991). As is hinted at in the previous extracts, the data was as instructive in illustrating what permanent teachers considered 'real' teaching and teachers (i.e., themselves) to be, as it was in providing explanatory frameworks for supply work.

Supply teachers were seen as part of the solution to a problem where less desirable alternatives were excessive work loads for permanent staff, split classes, and worst of all, sending children home. The most fulsome praise saw them described as 'gold dust' and 'saviours'. Paradoxically, they were also viewed as part of the problem, expressed in terms of availability, quality, administration, and cost (see Morrison in this volume). That paradox was expressed in terms of ambivalence and contradictions about supply teaching work. Words like 'flexible', 'resourceful', 'adaptable', and 'in control' were used by heads and teachers to describe essential qualities for supply teachers. Their work was recognized as potentially difficult, isolated, and onerous. At the same time it was viewed as the antithesis of what many primary teachers expected from teaching. A deputy head considered that a supply teacher should have:

> a good sense of discipline in the classroom. Our kids aren't easy. So I think a firm person who is going to stand no nonsense. A sense of humour . . . A good working knowledge, not just filling in time to pass the day, giving them bits of paper to draw on.

She went on to distance herself from the role:

> I wouldn't do it for any money . . . [For supply teachers] there's a nice freedom. When you've finished in the school for the day, there's nothing else. Some people like that. I wouldn't . . . not the uncertainty of what I'll be doing tomorrow, not knowing what the children were going to be like, not knowing any of their names.

An experienced class teacher 'positioned' herself in another way:

> I would imagine you would have to be fairly thick-skinned because you're always having to adapt your body language when you go into a school. You would also have to be fairly phlegmatic about people rushing in and saying 'didn't you know you weren't supposed to be doing that?'

MM: Could you envisage yourself becoming a supply teacher?

Teacher: Sometimes, but only when I'm desperate . . . I actually like what these people don't like . . . I actually like being involved with the class and with parents.

Equally interestingly, respect for the qualities a supply teacher needed to bring to the work were sometimes accompanied by low expectations of what could be achieved in the classroom. Dale Green opined:

> I think they [supply teachers] must be a genius. I couldn't do it . . .

Later:

> I'm a bit annoyed if they don't leave a note. I do expect that, but nothing else really. The odd day or even a week. I don't think it makes much difference.

Recent writers have applied the terms 'conscientiousness' and 'over-conscientiousness i.e., conscientiousness to a fault' to refer to current primary teaching work-loads (Campbell *et al*; 1991, p. 90). When applied to expectations of supply teachers and the preparations required to cover teacher absence, the term was reflected upon in a variety of ways. Some teachers considered it their responsibility to leave detailed work plans for supply teachers; others expected supply teachers to come prepared with their own work schedules. Indeed, in the case of short-term absence, several teachers considered that independent approaches brought advantages; this was expressed in terms of 'fresh' or 'different' attitudes to children's learning. Among those who prepared detailed work schedules for supply teachers, were those who expected them to 'give something of themselves', to be firm disciplinarians, and to 'like kids'. In Centrelink it was accepted practice for work records to be left for returning teachers; a common response to this practice was, however, less discernible and at the discretion of the returning teacher. In the following instance a teacher was asked to explain what happened when he returned after absence:

> I ask the children what they did . . . Generally I'll just carry on as if I hadn't been away. Depends on if they've done work I've set in between, and then we just carry on, it's easy. But if they've done something a bit different it's basically ignore what the supply teacher has been doing. We'll just carry on as if there hadn't been a break.

From the above it would appear that supply teachers were considered effective when they enabled classteachers to return and carry on where they had left off (one interviewee described this in terms of 'keeping the class ticking over'). Thus, part of their value might be seen in terms of neutralizing adverse effects of permanent teacher absence, in effect rendering invisible supply teachers' contributions. Discarding work done in the teacher's absence was a practice referred to in teacher and pupil interviews, and reinforces that invisibility.

Clearly there is a difference in the qualitative effect on a child's education of a teacher's absence of say, two days, known in advance, and an absence of six weeks or more, where the substitute teacher may be one or more teachers unfamiliar with the school. This was recognized by permanent and substitute teachers. Generally, both welcomed opportunities to discuss work, either before or after the cover period. Though the nature of supply work made this relatively uncommon, this was occasionally possible when absence was pre-planned, as for example, in relation to absence for in-service training. As expected, comments by senior managers were more closely focused upon organizational issues, and the match between expectation and reality.

Heads and Deputies Talking

Because recent educational and financial changes had increased school management tasks, it would have been surprising not to find heads' perceptions about supply cover linked to organizational issues. An interviewee with supply cover responsibilities commented on headteachers' expectations:

> Although there are exceptions . . . what the headteacher wants [from the supply teacher] is that there's no hassle, he doesn't want parents up complaining, he doesn't want rowdy children, he doesn't want people flying out of the room . . . he doesn't want you knocking on his door and saying 'I can't control so-and-so' . . . he or she doesn't really want to know you're there.

With the introduction of the National Curriculum it was recognized that expectations were changing. The interviewee continued:

> There are some heads who say I don't want you doing your own thing at all . . . in these days of the National Curriculum . . . everything will be programmed for them.

Whilst regular in-service training for supply team members focused increasingly on National Curriculum issues, there was some regret among the supply team that the hallmarks of effective supply teaching — its spontaneity and independent approaches to children's learning — were being gradually eroded. Primary school heads were asked to outline qualities sought in supply teachers. Organizational issues for schools were interwoven with discussion about professional attributes like adaptability, flexibility, and control. John Astley, headteacher of Tower Primary School, responded in the following way:

> I haven't any pre-conceived ideas about supply teachers ... I can understand why there are pre-conceived ideas, 'if they are good enough teachers why can't they get a full-time job in school' and things like that ... There is a certain inevitability about the situation ... stress ... teachers are cracking up more easily now than ever before ... I can't make any pre-judgments in that situation when I know I have the need for [supply teachers] and they are the best solution to the problems I have in school.

What qualities was Frank Sims, head of Longbricks Primary School looking for?

> Frank Sims: Well, in all honesty ... where I'm under a reasonable amount of pressure, truthfully I'm looking for someone who can go into the classroom and essentially keep the class in good order, in the very old-fashioned sense ... On my better days, when the pressures aren't so evident I'm looking for somebody who's going to come in and become involved with the children because the children in this school come from fairly deprived backgrounds ... I actually want to see supply teachers attempting to teach and not just discipline. So it sounds a little contradictory, but do you get my drift?

Linking staffing to curriculum matters, Frank Sims continued:

> Theoretically, supply teachers are meant to be able to just swan into a school and just pick up the National Curriculum. It can't be done but at least they're doing their best ... With the best will in the world, unless it's a long-term placement, I still see them as essentially a holding exercise ... unless you get an exceptional person, there's not much enrichment from my pupils' point of view. Unless someone comes in and fills the school with sunshine, which does happen occasionally.

Marlene Morrison

For headteacher Janet Dean, access to an established supply team and LEA supply register had facilitated a process of school merger, and allowed teachers involved to cope with 'the stress and trauma . . . suffer [ed] during an amalgamation'. Being 'a heavy user' of supply had been part of a deliberate strategy to encourage cohesion of school policy and practice. This allowed staff release for planning and professional development, and enabled senior managers to focus on key management tasks. Confidence in the ability of supply teachers to develop children's learning was critical:

> Janet Dean: I certainly think my choices would have been restricted if I didn't know that what I was getting was going to be quality [supply cover] . . . If I'd had to shop around and look at people willy nilly I don't think I might have gone down that road.

(Subsequent exploration revealed that not all staff were committed to the strategy outlined. This was linked to the need for improved staff communications, and concerns about continuity of children's learning. On occasion, supply teachers became targets for the verbal 'off-loading' of such concerns, making visible another largely hidden dimension to supply teachers' work.)

Heads interviewed had opted into supply arrangements whereby they paid an annual charge for access to a centrally maintained system. Relative advantages and disadvantages in using casual and supply team cover were discussed. A deputy head considered that:

> In an ideal world a supply teacher would go into a class and carry on education seamlessly. This is not an ideal world, so basically you operate on the principle that you do your best for the children . . . the casual supply list offers a greater opportunity because you can actually pick people who are fairly closely matched to the teacher *or* have an expertise that you know the [class] teacher does not have . . . all this will hopefully by the end of [children's] school career, balance out.

With the supply team:

> you get whoever is supplied so you do not have any control of that. The lack of control is a problem . . . The down side is that a casual supply can say *no* . . . if the [supply team] are told to go somewhere they have to say *yes* . . . That is crucial because

we have had difficulties with a particular class . . . which has a reputation of being somewhat undisciplined . . . the problem is that the rumour gets round . . . A number of supply teachers, and I know this for a fact, will on principle say 'whose class is it?' and if I say it's a particular class will say *no* . . . now if that problem became endemic then we would have a great problem.

Several important issues are raised here. First, classes or schools which experienced most difficulties in obtaining supply teachers were those most dependent on an LEA system. Second, whilst this facilitated availability and quality of cover, it could not guarantee the same person. Continuity of cover, therefore, did not necessarily mean consistency of approach or of teacher. Third, in the absence of centrally organized schemes, some schools would become doubly disadvantaged, in competition for staff with schools in areas where both regular and supply teachers might prefer to work. Finally, all of the above depended upon the availability of a reserve labour pool willing and able to be used at short notice.

So far, much of the discourse about supply teaching has referred to understandings among permanent staff. Attention is now drawn to self-identities and the views and experiences of supply teachers themselves.

Self-images

Anecdotal descriptions of the supply teacher suggest a stereotype of the woman teacher who is primarily occupied in domestic and child-care responsibilities. Certainly the supply work force is predominantly female, but the research challenged the stereotype of 'Mrs-so-and-so'. As is shown, this becomes more complex where perceptions about commitment and involvement were used to distinguish supply teachers from their professional colleagues. A wide range of people did supply work, for diverse reasons. During the primary school case studies the author met eight supply teachers working in schools. Of the five female and three male supply teachers, three worked on the supply team and five were listed on the casual supply register. Two team members worked full-time, and one part-time. The rest worked intermittently on a full or part-time basis. One supply teacher was contracted to work part-time in one school, and on a casual basis in others. Of the eight teachers, two combined teaching with child-care

53

responsibilities; one faced the problem of a child with recurring health problems. Jane, for example, aimed to return to full-time teaching 'within four to five years' and considered that her current work enabled her 'to keep in touch'. She contrasted her position to those of colleagues who had taken 'complete breaks' and were, for a variety of reasons, 'finding their return difficult'. Doing supply work had made her conscious of the need for specific short-term teaching strategies; she had been unaware of these when teaching full-time. Key issues included getting 'an instant measure of the class' as well as gaining respect and control, sometimes 'on a daily basis'.

Dorothy was supply teaching because she 'had been asked'. A retired teacher, she found herself in regular demand. She liked 'feeling useful' but considered she had less patience than previously and reflected on the need to continually 'revise [her] discipline standards downwards'. Modest about her overall effect on children's learning, her main aim was 'to foster a love of reading'. Like Dorothy, several supply teachers felt they had specific contributions to make in the classroom.

Russ was in the middle of what he considered to be a lateral move within education:

> We'd got young children . . . a baby at home . . . I just wanted a mid-term career break from that so that my wife and I would be able to carry on working.

Previously in school management:

> I wanted a bit of time out to do what I enjoy doing which is teaching children.

He considered supply work to have broadened his experience:

> It's given me a lot of opportunity to evaluate the strengths and weaknesses of the way management works in different schools . . . whether I choose to return to educational management or whether I will be looking at some specialist off-shoot, that's really something to be decided over the next couple of years.

For three supply teachers, supply teaching was integral to life schedules which included more than one occupational role. In each case, supply work was subsidiary employment. For a youth worker and a writer an interest in children's education provided a link between occupational roles. For the supply teacher who worked full-time on the supply team, supply work was currently central to her career interests. A move to Centrelink had resulted from the relocation of her husband's business. An experienced teacher, supply teaching was seen initially as a necessity rather than choice. She now valued the 'variety' and 'satisfaction' in her work, and was not seeking a return to employment in one school.

It might be expected that the reasons which motivated teachers to do supply work would be reflected both in self-images and experiences of supply teaching. In the following extract, a supply teacher uses experience of both regular and supply teaching to explore the likely impact of short-, medium-, and long-term placements upon his identity as a teacher and upon children's learning:

> If it were literally a question of a day or so then you're not going to pretend you're going to have a massive impact . . . if you're given a free rein and free choice you hope you will come up with . . . ideas that you know will spark the children.

In the case of long-term absence, 'you operate totally as a classteacher'. This included planning, marking and recording children's work, and attending parent and staff meetings. The most challenging placement was felt to be the period between short and long term, where the duration of absence remained uncertain and/or where the class might have already experienced more than one supply teacher. This was seen as:

> a little bit tricky because I would not wish to try and totally reorganize a classroom situation. So I would feel under a degree of constraint not to necessarily organize things in the way you would wish to . . . it's a bit of a balancing act really.

Constraints attendant upon these kinds of 'balancing acts' and a sense of 'half-way' belonging, were, on occasion, compounded by attitudes among some permanent colleagues. Most supply teachers had worked full-time in the past and may have shared those attitudes. Whilst experience had enabled them to reconsider substitute teachers' skills, it was interesting to note that a minority retained views acquired earlier in their careers:

> William: Well I think it's childminding . . . unfortunately . . .
> I've got a particular interest in [a specific area of the primary

Marlene Morrison

wanted to collect their word-books. Kay permitted this, but kept the door open in order to keep an eye on the children, who entered a classroom across the corridor.

There was consternation as the bell sounded for morning break. Kay was unaware that at this school children finished their tasks five minutes before break in order to eat tuck. Eating was not permitted in the playground. Kay promised to allocate five minutes after break for the children to eat. This satisfied most of the children who then left the classroom. Kay found herself surrounded by a group of children unsure about how to use their recent purchases. Half the break period was used to show the children how to operate yo-yos. This gave Kay only a few minutes in the staffroom, enough time to ask whether she could 'use any cup'. Two staff members said hello and asked her what class she was covering. A sign on the wall read WE WELCOME ALL WHO ENTER HERE INCLUDING SUPPLY.

The author rejoined Kay at lunchtime in the staffroom where she met the teacher whose class she was covering in the afternoon. He was going to a pupil-transfer meeting at the local secondary school, and had left instructions and materials for his year 6 class who would be continuing their topic work on the Victorians. Two children, Paul and Petra, had been given individual work programmes.

Afternoon registration took place. Paul and Petra had been instructed previously to sit alone on opposite sides of the classroom. Petra looked fretful and isolated. Kay's strategy was to move around the room, helping children to locate information, suggesting approaches to layout and design, and occasionally loaning a rubber or pencil sharpener. She maintained the same friendly interest in Paul and Petra's work. Cooperating with a 'new' teacher appealed to Petra; she approached Kay at regular intervals, seeking reassurance that she was 'doing the work right'. Paul was on task when he thought he was being observed; otherwise he daydreamed. Across the gap between his table and a group work table, his friend Tom tried to disturb him whenever Kay was working with others. They practised rude signs when her back was turned. Showing considerable speed and dexterity, the signs disappeared when Kay moved in their direction. Tom listened attentively when Kay offered assistance at his group table.

Mid-afternoon and with a quiet hum of activity in the room, the deputy head entered. Kay confirmed that the children were working well. From her resource bank she had more materials available should the class complete their topic work before the end of the afternoon. At the end of the day she returned briefly to the staffroom to collect her case, and to the office to get her form signed. Notwithstanding the presence of an observer, she considered that the day had been fairly typical.

In Retrospect

Kay Porter did not identify herself primarily as 'a teacher', but remained confident about her ability to teach on a supply basis. Devoting much of her energy and talent to a career outside teaching, she used some of both to tap into a subsidiary role which offered supplementary financial and personal rewards. Working mainly in isolation from teaching colleagues, she welcomed brief contacts with professionals, but confirmed her identity as supply teacher with children in the classroom rather than with adults. Children's attitudes, behaviour, and responsiveness became the 'critical reality definers' (Riseborough, 1985). Events like assemblies, for example, were described by her as 'disruptions' to teaching strategies she tried to develop in the classroom.

She remained realistic about what was achievable in terms of children's learning, sharing with permanent teachers concerns about classes which had experienced successive supply teachers:

> I've been to schools where classes have had five teachers in a year for various reasons. It's just a mish mash of people coming in and it must be very disruptive for the class and for the school.

Part of her self-image was sustained by a belief that there needed to be closer ties between youth work, leisure, and schooling; this was linked to her personal route into supply teaching.

> I was approached by a school in the area. I was at a management committee meeting at a youth club. The local headmistress was at it and said it's a shame we don't have much relations between youth work, leisure and schools. And I said, Ah! well, actually I've done all three . . . and we got together, and she offered me part-time casual supply.

Observing Kay in action reinforced earlier comments about the need for supply teachers to be adaptable, resourceful, flexible, and in control. As importantly, observation provided a reminder that opportunities to use such qualities depended also on the 'invisible presence' of regular teachers and the situational contexts in which supply teachers operated. Access to one school day in the life of Kay Porter allows only a brief glimpse into some of the complexities of supply teaching. Considered alongside other data, however, it offers several insights into supply work and teacher identities.

First, it suggests that teaching, including supply, is not a monolithic art or set of skills. It is created and adapted to the needs of different children, different schools, and a variety of teaching situations. Supply work takes place in classrooms which have already been disturbed by the absence of usual teacher(s) and routine(s).

Second, whilst teaching retains a core of common characteristics, the nature of supply work and its situational constraints reinforces the need for specific strategies and skills, for example, the management of teacher entry into the classroom and coping with routines which may be more familiar to the children than to the teacher. As long as teacher absence is discussed as aberrant and atypical, these kinds of short-term teaching strategies remain hidden, even denied.

Third, in common with other forms of teaching, supply work can be characterized by creativity or by mediocrity. Mediocrity can be compounded by low expectations of what is achievable in the classroom; creativity remains partly hidden either because the outcomes of supply work are ignored when the usual teacher returns, or because the very distinctive skills of keeping a class 'ticking over' remain undervalued and under-researched.

Fourth, as with all teaching (Woods, 1990, p. 13), the personal qualities of supply teachers are part of the total activity known as supply work. For example, in the observational account, Kay Porter's approach to supply teaching was as much an extension of her own qualities and approach to teaching as it was a feature of supply work. This, in turn, is affected by issues of time, physical and professional isolation, an absence of specific school-based information, and the expectations of permanent colleagues. As is shown, expectations can be ambiguous and contradictory, and interlaced with understandings about 'real' or 'proper' teaching.

Fifth, supply teachers' self-identities are sustained and adapted as part of a complex mix of motivating factors. In some cases, substitute teaching exposes professionals to potential conflicts between values and identities established in earlier teaching careers and the day-to-day realities of supply work ('it's just baby-sitting'). Survival strategies include those which prioritize self-identities outside teaching. Paradoxically, supply work enables some participants to concentrate on what they consider to be the core of teaching, namely the daily interactions between teacher and children in classroom settings. Freed from the bureaucratic constraints of school organizations, they are joined by another group whose intermittent teaching experiences allow them to retain a sense of shared identity and competence between personal and professional lives. For those in the latter group, supply teaching is either a staging post for entry or re-entry into permanent teaching or, as in the case of retired teachers, part of a gradual rather than abrupt loss of occupational identity and income.

Conclusion

Supply teachers are playing an increased role in many schools. Relatively little is known about these teachers, their approaches, or the contexts in which they work. Nias considers that:

> what all the characteristics of teaching have in common is their capacity to affect the individual teacher's self-image. (Nias, 1989, p. 105)

This chapter has explored some of the ways in which the characteristics of supply work are being interpreted by supply teachers and their permanent colleagues. A specific example has drawn attention to situational context and experience. Central to the exploration has been an interest in supply teacher identities from the perspectives of individuals and 'significant others', and an understanding of the teacher 'self', whether permanent and temporary. This is interwoven with the multiplicity of situations in which supply teachers currently operate.

To date, much of the imagery about supply work and supply teachers has been dominated by those who are permanent and full-time stakeholders in education. In current financial and educational contexts, the future of teacher substitution remains uncertain. This chapter takes some initial steps in giving a voice to those who, paradoxically, remain both peripheral and central to understandings about teacher substitution.

Note

1 This was part of a research project funded by the Leverhulme Trust, entitled Supply Teaching in English Schools: an investigation of policy, processes and people. Conducted by R.G. Burgess, S. Galloway, M. Morrison, it was based at the Centre for Educational Development, Appraisal and Research (CEDAR) at the University of Warwick.

References

BALL, D. (1972) 'Self and identity in the context of deviance: the case of criminal abortion' in SCOTT, R. and DOUGLAS, J. (Eds) *Theoretical Perspectives on Deviance*, New York, Basic Books.

BROWN, S. and EARLEY, P. (1990) *Enabling Teachers to Undertake Inservice Education and Training*, Slough, NFER for the DES.

CAMPBELL, R.J., EVANS, L., S.R. ST. J. NEILL, and PACKWOOD, A. (1991) *Work Loads, Achievement and Stress*, London, AMMA.

COOLEY, C. (1902) *Human Nature and The Social Order*, 1983 ed., New Brunswick, New Jersey, Transaction Books.

DAVIES, B. and HARRÉ, R.C. (1991) 'Positioning: the discursive production of selves', in *the Journal of the theory of social behaviour*, 20,1.

DAVIS, F. (1965) 'The Cab-driver and his fare: facets of a fleeting relationship' in POTTER, D. and SARRE, P. (Eds) (1974), *Dimensions of Society: a reader*, Milton Keynes, Open University Press.

GALLOWAY, S. (1993) 'Out of Sight, Out of Mind': a response to the literature on supply teaching', in *Educational Research*, 35, 2, Summer.

GOFFMAN, E. (1959) 'Presentation of Self to Others', in POTTER, D. and SARRE, P. (Eds) (1974) *Dimensions of Society: a reader*, Milton Keynes, Open University Press.

HUGHES, E.C. (1951) 'Work and the Self', in ROHRER, J.H. and SHERIF, M. (Eds) *Social Psychology at the Crossroads*, New York, Harper and Row.

LOVEYS, M. (1988) 'Supplying the Demand? Contract, mobility, and institutional location in the changing world of the supply teacher' in OZGA, J. (Ed.) (1988) *School Work: Approaches to the Labour Process of Teaching*, Milton Keynes, Open University Press.

MEAD, G.H. (1934) *Mind, Self and Society*, Chicago, University of Chicago Press.

MORRISON, M. (1991) 'The Language of Supply: a shifting interface for LEAs, schools and supply teachers', Paper presented at the BERA Conference, Nottingham Polytechnic, August.

MORRISON, M. (1993) 'Running for Cover: Substitute teaching and the secondary curriculum', in *Curriculum*, 14, 2, pp. 125–139.

MORRISON, M. and GALLOWAY, S. (1993) 'Researching Moving Targets: using diaries to explore supply teachers' lives, Paper presented at the British Sociological Association Conference University of Essex, 5–8 April to be published in the selection of conference papers.

NIAS, J. (1988) 'What it means "to feel like a teacher": the subjective reality of primary school teaching' in OZGA, J. (Ed.) *School Work: Approaches to The Labour Process of Teaching*, Milton Keynes, Open University Press.

NIAS, J. (1989) *Primary Teachers Talking: A Study of Teaching as Work*, London, Routledge.

RISEBOROUGH, G. (1985) 'Pupils, teachers' careers, and schooling: an empirical study' in BALL, S. and GOODSON, I. (Eds) *Teachers' Lives and Careers*, Lewes, The Falmer Press.

SALAMAN, G. (1975) 'Occupational Categories and Cultures: an introduction' in ESLAND, G., SALAMAN, E. and SPEAKMAN, M. (Eds) *People and Work*, Milton Keynes, Open University Press.

SHILLING, C. (1991) 'Supply Teachers: working on the margins: A Review of the Literature', in *Educational Research*, 33, 1, Spring, pp. 3–11.

SHILLING, C. (1992) 'Reconceptualising Structure and Agency in the Sociology of Education: structuration theory and schooling', in *the British Journal of the Sociology of Education*, 13, 1.

SIKES, P., MEASOR, L. and WOODS, P. (1985) *Teachers' Careers: Crises and Continuities*, Lewes, The Falmer Press.

TROTTER, A. and WRAGG, E. (1990) 'A Study of Supply Teachers', in *Research Papers in Education*, 5, 3, pp. 251–76.

WOODS, P. (1990) *Teacher Skills and Strategies*, London, The Falmer Press.

constraints for teachers — the availability of time (McCormick and James, 1983; Newton, 1989).

Supply Planning

The relatively long lead-time for an undertaking such as 'Project day' allows a number of issues to be addressed where supply teachers are to be employed to cover for members of the teaching staff. For example, one is able to give consideration to the subject(s) involved, the nature and level of the work, and the possibility of matching these with the specialisms of the supply staff available. Similarly, one can give due weight to supply teachers' familiarity with the school, and the nature and characteristics of the teaching group(s) to be covered, and how this might be organized to match the strengths and skills of the supply staff to be employed. Whether new to the school or familiar with it, supply staff can be advised in advance of the timetable to be covered and, where possible, given some idea of the work to be done. Knowing why a class's regular teacher is absent, particularly in a case like this, provides the opportunity for a positive interchange between supply staff and pupils alongside dialogue about the business of the lesson. Equally important, the issue of continuity can be addressed: where heads of curriculum area, for example, join a primary day conference on site on a rolling basis throughout the day, one of the parameters built into the organization of their release can be the need to avoid covering any group of pupils more than once.

The same criterion can be applied to the blocks of time made available on different days for departmental evaluation and follow-up meetings. Where the same teaching group is affected over a more extended period of time — the class, for example, of a year 7 coordinator involved in the project — then continuity is often found through a supply teacher familiar with the school and with the class, and sometimes involved with the pupils on a regular basis throughout the year.

Continuity and Time

The ability to make arrangements which maximize the benefits to be derived from the availability of a 'pool' of skilled personnel, and minimize (though they do not eliminate) the disruption caused to pupils' education, allows an acceptable balance to be struck, where developments which the school considers a priority in the short-, medium- or long-term interests of its pupils are undertaken. In the same way, for example, an education–industry liaison initiative between Mandeville School and the Rover Group at Cowley, Oxford, with curriculum development as its focus, saw thirteen members of staff seconded on a rolling basis, and for different lengths of time, over a two-year period from 1986, each teacher working to a common curricular brief. Rover personnel, school staff and students worked together at Mandeville and at Rover, with results which continue to be visible in the school. Education–industry initiatives have also been one way in which we have sought to enhance the academic-vocational balance in the sixth-form curriculum, with the introduction of a BTEC (Business and Technology Education Council) first in 1992, and a BTEC National projected for 1994. Members of staff have been able to update their industrial/commercial experience, for example, and design student assignments in conjunction with business partners. These projects, like others before and after them, including our current participation in 'Compact' arrangements, owe an important part of their shape and size — their quality — to the availability of good supply staff able to release teachers — over the short or medium term — for key activities.

Paradoxically, while the development and evaluation of particular initiatives take staff out of school periodically, their successful implementation will often rely heavily on continuity of contact between those same teachers and their pupils. This is a circle which can only be squared by the careful management of time on the one hand, and the creation of some continuity on the other by, for example, the use of staff teams with common expertise and experience, and carefully briefed supply. Our early unfamiliarity with the pedagogy of the Certificate of Pre-Vocational Education (CPVE), for instance, made the existence of a course team invaluable in coping as a staff with the level and volume of training and coordination required in the first eighteen months. The ability of one or two supply teachers, familiar with the school and aware of the style of work in the CPVE 'base room', to stand in when required was equally valuable.

The same can be said for the way in which supply staff facilitate developments with particular structural implications. At Mandeville, for example, pupil progress is reported to parents through a Record of Achievement. Pupil participation and negotiation is an integral part of the process and this factor, among others, makes time a critical constraint for all members of staff, but particularly for form tutors. Part of our response is to re-affirm the smallest practicable tutor-group sizes as a matter of policy; another has been to create an 'RoA week', when each period 3 (daily) over a week in March has been dedicated to RoA work in tutor groups. As a consequence of this policy, there are certain, predictable occasions when the internal availability of staff for cover may be quickly exhausted and the school moves, also as a matter of policy, to employ supply staff, and preferably those with some prior experience of working, in this instance, with the Mandeville RoA. The school would persist with this staff deployment and organization of tutor groups were supply staff not available: the policy has an educational *raison d'être* and a net administrative advantage. However, while it has not been adopted because supply staff are available, it has been adopted in the knowledge that that resource exists.

Thus, as far as developmental work is concerned, and as the examples described above have attempted to show, an important contributory factor to the quality of what is achieved is the creation of time for school staff to plan, prepare, review, and follow through. In this respect, the supply teacher plays a key role. And what is true of developmental work is also true of a teacher's central role: day-to-day classroom teaching. We have become sufficiently convinced at Mandeville of the link between time and quality on the one hand, and lesson cover as a prime cause of stress on the other, to include this year in our annual review of the staff-cover policy the possibility of employing supply from the first day of staff absence through illness, rather than after the third day which has been our normal practice to date. Our analysis shows that such a decision (possible now under LMS) is likely to be cost-effective, comparing favourably, for example, with annual premiums to insure against staff absence. The professional commitment of Mandeville staff, as elsewhere, in minimizing personal absence due to illness — or any other reason — is also a critical factor in making this reconsideration possible. Some careful safeguards, of course, will need to be built in: what level of cover required, for example, on any individual or combination of teaching timetables will activate the policy? And its implementation will need to be carefully monitored: will the benefits we anticipate for staff and pupils, for example, be significantly offset because cover teaching is predominantly by external supply rather than permanent members of staff? Only careful evaluation of any change in policy will provide us with a reliable answer in the Mandeville context.

Availability

It is easier to be sanguine about achieving an acceptable balance between disruption to pupils' learning on the one hand, and the benefits to be derived from developmental work on the other, when decisions concerning the volume, pace and timing of change lie with the school. It is less easy when responding to external agendas. We are fortunate at Mandeville in working with a number of supply staff who, when necessary, will operate as flexibly as possible. There remains, however, a problem with regard to accessing that resource in the context of, for example, teacher appraisal: how does one cover a teacher carrying out one of the two statutorily required thirty-minute (minimum) classroom-observation sessions? A number of options are available; however, some compromise important components of the developmental rationale for appraisal; some generate a disproportionate administrative work-load in attempting an equitable 'pay-back' to members of staff who cover during their non-contact time. All of the options, notwithstanding cooperative supply staff, present significant problems.

It is also easier to be sanguine about the employment of supply staff when those staff are, in fact, available. At Mandeville, as commonly happens elsewhere, we work with a relatively small number of regular supply staff, (although the composition of the group tends to change year-to-year, and the level of demand for cover periodically sees a larger number of less familiar faces in the staffroom). The development of a regular commitment has a number of important mutual advantages for school and supply staff alike. Familiarity with policies, procedures and practice, with the physical layout of the school, and with departmental idiosyncracies for example, together with some acquaintance with members of staff and knowledge of classes and pupils, tend to make for a more manageable, satisfying and productive day. This is an important consideration. The supply teacher in a familiar school is faced with a number of challenges on a regular basis: when to use discretion in releasing a child from the classroom, for example, and how to discover if that expectation of pupil behaviour really has changed since the last time in school. How much more difficult the situation is when organizational and procedural uncertainties are added.

Training

An invitation to regular supply staff to participate in appropriate INSET activities can also offer a number of mutual advantages. The opportunity for the individual supply teacher to update her or his knowledge of National Curriculum subject developments, for example, is of obvious benefit. This option, however, is complicated by a

Malcolm Newton

number of considerations. Cost constraints mean that the invitation is likely to be only to sessions where no (significant) additional expenditure is incurred from the school's Grants for Educational Support and Training (GEST) budget; and for the same reason, no payment is likely to be offered for attendance at a training day. A supply teacher may, in any case, be unwilling to commit such a day, understandably, in that it represents the potential loss of a day's earnings. Equally, personal commitments, or simply the problem of 'getting over in time' from another school, make twilight sessions problematic. As a single institution, with a staff development programme closely geared to our own training needs, we also find (perhaps surprisingly) that relatively little of our 'accessible' programme is sufficiently relevant to the individual needs of supply staff to justify their commitment to it. As GEST budgets at the centre contract, and leave LEAs unable to offer the training to supply staff they might wish to consider, there is a need to review how supply staff can gain access to relevant training and development. If there is to be no budget for this purpose at the centre, perhaps self-interest (if nothing else) suggests that schools should consider making a combined, cooperative offer coordinated, for example, through the LEA.

Expertise and Quality

The ability of the school to locate supply staff is significantly enhanced by the operation in each of this LEA's four administrative areas of a 'supply list'. These are updated and circulated to schools on a regular basis, giving contact details for each person offering to do supply work, together with information about phase and subject specialism(s) as appropriate. Inclusion on the list normally follows receipt of references after application to the area education office, and interview either at area by the officer responsible or in school by senior member(s) of staff. This last alternative at Mandeville usually involves the senior teacher responsible for staff cover, together with another member of the senior management team on a rolling basis. The 'supply list' is a crucial source of information. Although very difficult to keep completely accurate, as people move in and out of the area for example, it offers a range of further contacts when a school's own local network is exhausted. Equally important is the information it offers about the pool of expertise and experience which exists locally, and the potential interest of the people it represents in taking up longer-term commitments in school, on either a part-time or full-time, temporary or permanent basis.

It is also possible to be sanguine about the employment of supply when staff whom the school considers suitable are available. In conversation with colleague headteachers from primary and special schools recently, we shared some expectations of the professional and personal qualities that would characterize an effective supply teacher. At the conclusion of our discussion it came as no real surprise that they were all qualities intrinsic to any good teacher, with perhaps some changes of emphasis. The quality of the children's classroom experience was our first concern. Thus, we should prefer to employ staff who are prepared to teach, as opposed to 'child-mind' a class. This does not necessarily mean being a specialist in any given area, but it does mean engaging with the work set for the group, offering information, advice and guidance to pupils and, if necessary, logging for the returning teacher problems and topics which supply and class between them have been unable satisfactorily to resolve. In this approach to lesson cover, we saw the best opportunity for the supply teacher to establish positive relationships with the group as a whole, and with individual pupils; and thereby, a way too of anticipating and pre-empting problematic behaviour by pupils, some of whom will be unsettled simply by facing a different and, possibly, unknown teacher. For the same reasons, a supply teacher needs to be alert to the needs of a group, and active in responding to them, moving around the classroom as necessary rather than remaining stationary or seated for long periods. How she or he responds to challenging behaviour is also important: a repertoire of graduated responses, all of which are controlled, reasonable and firm, is one description of good practice. First and foremost, then, it is essential that a supply teacher is a skilled classroom practitioner.

Specialism

Clearly, there are advantages if the supply teacher is also a specialist in the curriculum area(s) to be covered. In addition to a specialist input to the class it would mean, for example, that, alongside any written tasks, some form of practical work could be undertaken in, say, science and craft design technology, and an interactive oral approach pursued in modern languages. This ability to make significant progress with a programme of study, and maintain a department's pedagogic style is, in our experience, of clear benefit to the children. It can also offer a simple, very practical bonus to members of staff whose lessons are being covered, in that they are likely to return to a class where momentum has not been seriously interrupted; and they do not face an excessive markload generated by their absence, and the need for the class to be 'kept busy'. It is for this sort of reason that departments at Mandeville will, where practical, re-organize to cover the classes of an absent colleague 'within the department' — as often at short notice as by prior arrangement. However, this 'subject match' between supply teacher and class is something we find very difficult to achieve on a short-term basis — i.e., when cover by supply staff is needed with little or no advance warning, usually because of illness, and probably only for one day.

There are a number of reasons for this. One is that the various specialisms are unevenly represented (or not represented at all) within the smaller group of regular supply staff at the school and across the broader spectrum of the LEA's supply list. Where particular specialisms are represented, the odds are normally very long against those particular individuals being available (at short notice) on the day required. Hence, at Mandeville certainly, the importance in this context of the skilled classroom practitioner who is able to operate as specialist occasionally, but more frequently as a good generalist. In addition, it is not unusual for the school to create a cover timetable for the day where supply staff will cover lessons in more than one curriculum area and for more than one teacher.

This may be because there is a simple 'fit' between two or more timetables; there may, alternatively, be a variety of internal arrangements in place for some of a teacher's classes; or it may be a deliberate 'mix and matching' of supply teacher and classes on the basis of their perceived compatibility. By contrast, we experience little difficulty in matching by phase and sector, i.e., supply staff trained for, and experienced in, mainstream secondary education. This is an advantage; though I suspect that we would be more prepared to welcome primary supply, for example, than they would be to respond to the opportunity to use their expertise in the secondary classroom. After a successful lesson, it was to a very complaisant year 10 class, for example, that Mrs Pickering, infant-trained, offered the invitation to 'go out and play' at morning break — to her own immediate discomfiture, but (what appeared to be) the group's corporate fond memory. Matching phase and sector, however, appears to be a greater problem for colleagues in special education and there, as elsewhere, the availability of a good generalist and practitioner, who is prepared to transfer and adapt their teaching skills to the particular needs of children in special schools, is an important factor.

Partnership

Many of the personal qualities which schools welcome in supply teachers will be apparent from what has already been said, particularly the need for flexibility. In addition, punctuality and reliability are key features; together with a pre-disposition to say 'yes' rather than 'no' when invited to come into school to cover. Resilience and stamina are also important: it takes a particular kind of strength, for example, to cancel over breakfast one set of arrangements for the day in favour of meeting eight groups of thirty children in a variety of rooms for a variety of subjects within the next five hours or so, a combination which can generate (whether or not one is familiar with the school) an infinite number of unknowns, and a consequential drain on energy and confidence. A sense of humour is an overworked phrase, but as apposite here as elsewhere. A sense of initiative is equally valuable: a contingency lesson 'in the bag' in case of emergency; adhesive name tags to help address pupils personally; a willingness to look for solutions to, rather than simply accept the consequences of, the organizational hiccoughs that happen in the best run establishments from time to time when temporary arrangements are in place. In addition, of course, there are issues to do with self-presentation, and the management of working relationships with colleagues — teaching and non-teaching — within the school.

Partners in a good — i.e., productive — working relationship have expectations of each other. If schools expect certain qualities and types of behaviour from supply staff working for them, it is only reasonable to expect schools to do what they can to enable a supply teacher to function as successfully as possible. Thus, giving as much notice as possible of a commitment has a number of advantages for school and supply staff alike. Arranging for the reception and briefing of supply staff in school is similarly more than a common courtesy, and assumes an established routine on the part of the school which accommodates new and regular supply teachers alike. The provision of adequate information and materials enables supply staff to find their way around. This last might take the form of a standard 'Welcome pack' for supply teachers containing, in addition to their timetable for the day:

- the timing and organization of the school day;
- the name, role and location of each member of staff, with key contacts/personnel highlighted, including:
  — arrangements for staff support;

- form-tutor list;
  - internal telephone numbers, and location of phones;
  - a map of the school, with any necessary explanation *re* buildings/sites/room numbering; and
  - tea/coffee/lunch arrangements for staff;
- essential routines, including, for example:
  - lesson registration and absence check;
  - authorization of release from classroom during lesson time;
  - emergencies: medical, fire, etc; and
  - pupil-movement rules; this section perhaps in the form of a precis of the school's behaviour policy and procedures;
- spare plain and lined paper, together with a set of pens and pencils;
- a salary claims form;
- a statement of the school's attitude towards supply staff including, for example, the possibility of participation in INSET; and
- a contents/index page.

On its return at the end of the day, consumables can be replaced, and the pack used again on a future occasion. Much of the information needed for such packs is likely to be readily available from a school's staff handbook; and although their initial composition and subsequent maintenance require some investment of time, this is likely to be recouped many times over in increased efficiency and better communication.

Managing Cover

A school's management of the staffing resource offered by a 'pool' of supply teachers is likely to fall to the member of staff responsible for staff cover. At the Mandeville School, this is a member of the senior management team (comprising headteacher, two deputy heads, and three senior teachers) and the responsibility is rotated, normally on an annual basis, among members of the team (excluding the headteacher).

The responsibility is shared partly for individual staff development purposes, partly for team-building purposes, and partly to share the very significant work-load it entails, which needs to be discharged in addition to other, very substantial commitments (including classroom teaching). The responsibility for staff cover has been retained within the senior team as we have seen the demand for staff time out of the classroom grow, and the relationship between decisions on staff release and school policies and priorities become ever more complex. Thus, in the context of a staff-cover policy, the senior member of staff in charge of cover will consider, in consultation with those responsible, the day-to-day impact of:

- school initiatives (such as those described at the beginning of this chapter);
- the implications of school-based and off-site INSET;
- internal and external moderation and standardization activities for GCSE and other examinations and tests;
- TVEI-related activity, including coordination and evaluation meetings;
- work with institutions of higher education on initial teacher training proposals;
- school journeys and visits;
- the release of staff to work with the LEA on issues of mutual interest and benefit (such as aspects of LMS);
- attendance at bodies such as the Standing Advisory Council on Religious Education;
- requests for pupil medical examinations;
- concurrent timetables, such as exam invigilation; and
- a range of other activities where the need to cover teacher absence can be predicted and planned for.

In the 1992–3 academic year, such commitments accounted for around 36 per cent of staff absence from lessons. Alongside these demands is the unpredictable incidence of staff absence through illness and for other personal reasons, where experience provides only the broadest of termly profiles. The member of staff in charge of cover, therefore, is regularly faced, often at short notice, with a range of decisions to make, some of which will involve a broad range of implications; most of which, over time, will have an important influence on the working conditions of her or his colleagues.

Developing and Reviewing Policy

The capacity of the school to arrange lesson cover internally is finite, not only in terms of the number of teachers available for this purpose at any particular time of the day, but also in terms of staff energy and morale. The school's cover policy, therefore, makes explicit the use of discretion in employing supply staff on those relatively infrequent occasions when absence clusters unavoidably around a particular day or half-day; or significant levels of cover are required over a protracted period of time. In this respect, the ability to respond quickly to local circumstances, enhanced by LMS, is of significant assistance; together with the efficient use of 'dedicated' funding, such as that available through GEST, TVEI, ITT, GCSE examination boards, and so on. Equally helpful is the willingness of some supply teachers to come into school for a part of the day only, when it would be impossible to justify their employment for longer. In these circumstances, as others, the school's priority is to achieve the optimum set of arrangements for pupils and staff alike, in order to maintain the quality of teaching and learning within the establishment. Cost is a secondary factor: important, of course, in terms of overall budget constraints and the need for sound judgment to be exercised but not, (unless by *force majeure*), as the lead criterion for action. The salary level of an individual supply teacher, for example, does not influence a decision as to whether or not she or he is called by the school: our criteria are suitability, and availability — and therein lies the auditor's 'value for money'.

The organization of staff cover is a time-consuming business. Notwithstanding the relatively favourable situation at Mandeville with regard to the availability of supply staff, it is not unusual for the responsible member of the senior team to spend the larger part of an evening telephoning different teachers in order effectively to set in place the arrangements — short — and long-term — required by the school. In addition, despite a set of school policies and procedures intended to facilitate the organization of cover on a day-to-day basis, the complexity of this exercise normally means that the teacher in charge of cover cannot give priority to any other activity until after the start of morning registration. Thereafter, there is a monitoring role to play, mediated if necessary through the school office, via messages to and from the teacher's classroom, by conversations at break and lunchtime, and by management by walking about. The role makes its own particular contribution to occupational stress. In designating a colleague, for example, to lose valuable non-contact time in order to cover, one knows the pressure and frustration that can be created as planned activities are rescheduled. Some of this disappointment can be offset by a range of coping strategies, of which humour is one. Cover slips in one establishment, for example, were known as 'bird droppings' between the sixth-formers who delivered them and the staff who received them in honour of the deputy who issued them; and as 'neutron bombs' when I succeeded him. At Mandeville, they become raffle tickets in a periodic 'prize draw'. Another strategy allows disappointment to be made explicit because it is directed against the conspiracy of circumstance rather than any individual. There is a corporate benefit to be derived from such strategies, as well as a personal benefit by the teacher in charge of cover. The role also has its own rewards, among them the satisfaction of working with good supply staff, and thereby making a particular contribution to staff welfare generally in the school.

If a cover system is as fair and equitable as possible, the open management of it should enhance its effectiveness. At Mandeville, the staff cover policy (see Appendix 2) is reviewed annually through the school's consultative procedures. In addition, an open record of the lessons covered by staff, on an individual and cumulative basis, is maintained. The criteria by which staff are asked to cover are also the subject of debate when the cover policy is reviewed. Thus, we have consistently decided that the discretion of the responsible member of the senior team is a better instrument to select who covers which lesson when, than the various alternatives available. Among the reasons for this is the importance attached to qualitative criteria — where a detailed knowledge of local circumstances is crucial — in addition to quantitative criteria. For their part, teachers in charge of cover need constant feedback (not normally in short supply) in addition to the annual review in order to evaluate the effects of the decisions they are taking. A school's policy and practice with regard to lesson cover will reflect the need to minimize discontinuity in pupils' learning; and to enable staff to respond to a growing agenda of initiatives and innovation which take them out of the classroom.

If the scene depicted at the start of this chapter lingers in the memory at Mandeville, it is in part because of the strategic support of supply staff. Schools will differ in their management of cover situations but in our experience attending to supply systems and relationships pays educational dividends.

References

McCormick, R. and James, M. (1983) *Curriculum Evaluation in Schools*, Croom Helm.

Newton, M.J. (1989) *Evaluation Strategies in School-Focussed Training*, CEDAR Reports No.4, Coventry, University of Warwick.

Chapter 6

Square Pegs and Round Holes: The Supply Coordinator's Role in Employing and Deploying Staff

Sheila Galloway

Who are the main actors in providing supply cover for secondary classes? Following the headteacher's account in Chapter 5, this chapter uses case study research to show how senior teachers in secondary schools balance the sometimes conflicting priorities that face them. It traces through a supply coordinator's decisions on cover as the school implements a central educational initiative while coping with staff absence. Taking us into classrooms to observe substitute teachers in action, the analysis teases out differences between specific curricular knowledge and general teaching skills. It argues that the largely invisible world of the supply teacher and the visible world of permanent teachers in schools are interdependent. The importance of the supply coordinator's role is structural, but management style and interpersonal relationships affect staff morale.

For 190 days each school year it is the supply coordinator who has most contact with supply teachers. The research on which this chapter draws[1] sought to record and explain aspects of the role and also to capture the reality behind the words of one supply teacher: 'There's no typical day on supply', a sentiment echoed by others. Clearly there is an infinite variety of LEA systems and school structures that shape supply provision: this chapter argues that studying school structures for teacher substitution together with the supply teacher at work reveals much about teaching, teachers and professional assumptions. As much, it is claimed, as research on 'regular' teaching reveals.

In considering on the one hand systems and structures and on the other interactions and relationships, there are two essential players: the school supply coordinator, and the supply teacher. Here the former is centre-stage, on the premiss that the locus of control at school level is the supply coordinator, who is also a part of the system herself or himself. She or he negotiates with others contacting new supply teachers, encouraging 'regulars' and maintaining relationships with colleagues. Every coordinator interviewed during this research project balanced an account of the school's procedure for organizing cover with observations that revealed how far those procedures depended on personnel-management skills and personal relationships with colleagues. Employing appropriate substitute teachers and deploying the professional skills available (from internal and external sources) is a complex activity. It relies on individual experience and takes place within institutional norms, but it is conducted in a changing world.

Leighton (1990) reminds us that traditionally teachers held specialist posts: 'one of the major characteristics of teachers' employment contracts has been their relative inflexibility' (op. cit., p. 134). Taking from Atkinson (1984) the view that the labour market can be seen in terms of 'core' and 'periphery', she notes the need for flexibility in the core work-force (in retraining, mobility and manning):

> Teachers do not equate in this regard. They have generally been appointed to specific schools and to specific areas of the curriculum. (ibid.)

However new contractual situations make the traditional securities attached to permanent posts much less certain than before. (Stenning, 1990; Buzzing, Morrison, and Lindley in this volume). Leighton too sees 'new complexities, increased fragmentation, and increased possibilities for tension' (Leighton, 1990, p. 134). Against this changing background for permanent teaching staff the supply coordinator employs temporary professional substitutes and allocates them to classes.

What Is a Supply Coordinator?

The term 'supply coordinator' is not commonly used in the secondary schools where we conducted case studies. It was adopted to avoid repeated reference in research accounts to 'the member of staff responsible for supply provision and cover'. Familiar titles such as 'curriculum coordinator', or 'INSET coordinator' support its use. In practice a member of the senior management team, usually a deputy head, does the job and sometimes on a list of staff duties it will simply be designated 'cover' or 'supply'. People speak of 'our supply person', or 'X does the timetable and cover'. So supply provision and cover overlaps and merges with other aspects of the deputy's job (Galloway, 1993a). This is often a virtue and ensures efficiency: the deputy who manages the programme of in-service training sees the need for emergency cover in relation to this. But the overlap can mean that tasks such as booking supply teachers or preparing daily-cover sheets may not be identified as 'supply' tasks, appearing to be simply related to 'managing INSET'. Invisibility in research studies and educational commentaries (Galloway, 1993b) is evident also in organizational structures. One indication is the way these tasks are easily merged with other duties.

In-depth research in four secondary schools tracked ways in which deputy heads handled supply issues. Their work varied with the nature of the school: its aims, staffing profile, intake, organization, and buildings. One senior teacher was developing databases to support budgetary control, and monitored weekly its use of external supply. The list of available supply teachers existed as a print-out, graded and colour-coded, indicating levels of preference. Another deputy's first lesson each day was a non-teaching period to ensure that immediate problems could be promptly dealt with. Secondary case studies included interviews and observation to flesh out the picture which is represented only sketchily by 'cover sheets' on a staff notice-board. In particular coordinators were observed planning the day's cover.

Data from one school are presented here against the overall framework developed in this research where supply issues are considered in terms of systems (at national, local and institutional levels) and also of interactions, between individuals or groups. To get close to the complex professional judgments being made, the chapter centres on Richardson School, a mixed 11–18 split-site comprehensive. (All people, institutions and authorities in this research project are given pseudonyms.) It covers both educational and organizational themes. The school's relationship with the LEA (here referred to as Medshire) is outlined in terms of the supply system, and against a backcloth of national imperatives. The data demonstrate mechanisms for putting teachers in front of classes. The supply coordinator makes critical judgments about who can best teach particular pupils, and why, and some of these judgments are reported, with their educational rationale. Finally, the coordinator is no mere administrator, but a manager of people, and the data show how one part of that dual role is to support staff and maintain morale. A glimpse is given of how the supply coordinator's decisions are enacted by supply teachers. (See Morrison and Galloway, 1993, for further examples.)

The backcloth to these organizational and educational tasks is a tapestry of events, some far distant, some in the foreground. If the warp of this cloth comprises initiatives and directives at the macro-level, the weft is the many programmes and events originating from within the school. Decisions may relate to macro-level policy or to micro-level decisions, or to both.

It would be helpful if this discussion could be located against other research on how schools manage supply, but this is scarce (Connor, 1993; Brown and Earley, 1990). Equally rare is reference to the daily activity that routinely takes much of a deputy's time (Hufferdine, 1992; Hulme, 1993). It would be wrong to generalize too freely from the specific data presented: there is no suggestion that the example given is typical or statistically representative. Nevertheless this case study is not at odds with other findings in this research. It uses a specific example to define certain processes and key features against which future analysis may continue: the narrowing of the focus provides greater depth in exploring critical themes. (See Bassey (1981) for a cogent discussion of generalization from case studies.) Particular elements out of line with overall trends in the project are noted.

Visible and Invisible Worlds

The focus is on the highly visible role of the supply coordinator. The data also show how far the visible activities of the institution depend upon an invisible world: that of the supply teacher. Supply teachers' lack of power is often noted (Trotter and Wragg, 1990; Shilling, 1991; Blackburne, Arkin, and Hackett, 1989) but in principle they collectively have the potential to jeopardize educational initiatives by choosing to be unavailable. If this paradox has not previously been discussed, it is perhaps because no such collectivity of supply teachers has to date been formed. Here the notion of latent conflict central to Lukes' (1974) analysis of power proves useful. In other ways too, our understanding of the interdependence of the visible and invisible worlds benefits from a 'three-dimensional' view of power, which

> allows for consideration of the many ways in which potential issues are kept out of politics, whether through the operation of social forces and institutional practices or through individuals' decisions. This, moreover, can occur in the absence of actual, observable conflict, which may have been successfully averted-though there remains here an implicit reference to potential

conflict. This potential, however, may never in fact be actualised. (Lukes, 1974, p. 24)

Supply coordinators and supply teachers are located in different worlds but the congruence of interest between them would seem to be easily demonstrable: the one solves an educational problem by employing the other. Coordinators are sensitive to supply teachers priorities: some will agree to late arrival in school for family reasons. (In this present case, deputy head Carol Brown, employing supply teacher Susan Bell, accepted that she was not available for a few hours each week when she worked at a sports centre.) Relationships are sustained by mutual recognition of pressing needs.

Coordinators have to accommodate the out-of-school priorities of these occasional employees. Other interests are not necessarily apparent in these negotiations, and Lukes leads us to question the obvious: 'What one may have here is a latent conflict, which consists in a contradiction between the interests of those exercising power and the real interests of those they exclude' (ibid.). To understand the visible and invisible worlds of supply we should ask also how far there is conflict or contradiction between these two worlds, and how far the interests of the parties do coincide. Using an alternative model (Atkinson, 1984), what tensions exist between core and periphery? As we try to explain educational policies and structures associated with the provision of cover and to trace whether such systems take account of the real interests of qualified teachers employed on an occasional basis, Lukes obliges us to look further: 'men's wants may themselves be a product of a system which works against their interests'. (op. cit., p. 34)

Macro-level Contexts and Micro-level Responses

Local Management of Schools

Autumn of 1991 saw many educational changes being implemented in English secondary schools. For Richardson it was early days in financial management, with staff mastering the devolved budget, and gaining experience in monitoring expenditure. Occasional and short-term contract staff were employed against this evolving situation.

Transitional relationships between central government and LEAs were resulting in reduced LEA activity as powers were devolved to schools. Some full-time supply teams were being disbanded. Medshire had never maintained a large team but the former complement of forty

The Supply Coordinator's Role in Employing and Deploying Staff

had reduced in recent years to ten. Schools in the county were used to relying on local contacts. The account below shows how it became imperative for the Richardson coordinator to find additional supply teachers.

Another transitional feature was a trial insurance scheme offered to schools covering the fourth to the twentieth days of a teacher's absence. Richardson School had not opted into this interim scheme, and felt the decision justified even after serious staff absence.

Schools and their Potential Intake

In other ways national contexts affected Richardson School. Recent educational reforms aimed to establish the accountability of the teaching profession, not least by new forms and styles of testing and communicating results. School-development plans were increasingly the blueprint for curriculum work and staff development and there was a sharper impetus for schools in a 'market economy' to ensure success (in some cases, survival) by maintaining a healthy intake, and attending to relations with local communities. One decision at Richardson, arising partly from discussion about examination results, had been to give extra time to heads of faculty and year to support staff as appropriate. The alternative approach of smaller teaching groups, (consequently more classes) was precluded by limited teaching spaces. In 1991–2 this allocation equalled three extra members of staff, on a full-time complement of 68.4 (in practice, seventy-five different teachers). Enhanced staffing to cover supply situations had not been discussed, but this was an additional resource (though technically provided for another purpose).

In relationships with the community, Richardson was fortunate. In a small market town, it had no immediate competitors, and took pupils from seven primary schools. Close to Medshire County boundary, it traditionally attracted pupils from a neighbouring County (almost 15 per cent of the intake in 1991–2). Location and size (1036 on roll in 1991–2) were in the school's favour and it had been comprehensive for almost twenty years. Historical links with a prestigious educational foundation, some attractive old buildings, and its status as the only secondary school in the town all contributed to its virtually unchallenged position, conveying the impression of a school with a past which was confident in its present role. School–home relations were rarely strained but the data show Carol Brown, the supply coordinator, aware that sixth-formers could be disadvantaged during lengthy staff illness, and that individual pupils might on occasion suffer an overload of substitute teachers:

> The other problem . . . is the child who that day has three supply teachers . . . I can't always monitor that child . . . because of the way the groups are . . .

> Occasionally I will get feedback from a parent who says, 'Miss Brown, I wasn't happy last week. My daughter had three supply teachers in three lessons and didn't want to come on Thursday because they said, 'What's the point? We haven't got a proper teacher.' Now that's the bit that worries me.

One teacher recalled in interview how pupils became 'disenchanted' with a build-up of staff absence the previous year:

> The kids have been very quick to let us know they are fed up with not having that subject taught to them.

A member of the senior management team pin-pointed the effects of staff absence for INSET:

> They begin to feel that in fact they are fairly low down [in] the priorities of the school . . . [This] is something on planning and something on courses that teachers go on. It's not actually them. And that's a bit of a demotivator, and I think the youngsters need to be — they in fact are — the most important thing. Teachers need to think that as well.

Though the difficulty of tracking particular pupils appeared intransigent, Miss Brown was always aware of it. Noticing one week that year 7 appeared to be hard hit by cover, she spoke to the principal about the reasons for this, in case parents should comment.

Overall Richardson School would seem well placed to implement national educational policies. The principal commented:

> The children . . . are quite amenable. You don't get major problems, though I'm not saying that all of the lessons a supply teacher takes will be as easy as blinking.

The Supply Coordinator's Role in Employing and Deploying Staff

Attracting suitable supply was only a serious problem at times of unprecedented illness or major initiatives.

Implementing a National Initiative

In the late 1980s secondary schools were responding to national and LEA guidelines on the introduction of Records of Achievement (RoA). Richardson staff had this on the INSET agenda during 1990–1, but progress had been slow, partly because of staff absence. With RoA interviews in October, further training became a priority: on a day in November tutors would have half-day release, with some requiring a whole day's cover. A mix of specialist and non-specialist substitutes enabled this training to take place and the example given below records one specialist supply teacher in action.

Local Features and Medium-term Problems

A feature of the school which affected both permanent and supply teachers was its two sites a few hundred yards apart. Years 7–10 were based at the west site, years 11–13 at the east site with sixth-form specialist rooms. For the supply teacher, a split site further complicates the series of unknowns that make up a working day. Carol Brown tried where feasible to 'block together' lessons at one site but

> there may well be some to-ing and fro-ing. It's not ideal and I try and avoid it but it does sometimes happen.

Short-term problems arise against medium-term uncertainties. Autumn had begun with the intermittent absence of a head of department covered by a supply teacher on the LEA list, and by other teachers in the department. Concurrent with this there was recurrent absence likely to lead to an early retirement. At this stage it was handled on an *ad hoc* basis. In considering the interpersonal skills that coordinators draw on, such situations merit attention. Less than clear-cut, they can be as demanding as those which present more obvious crises. One medium-term arrangement covered a maternity leave in craft and design which proved difficult. The solution was an instructor with a degree who had no teacher training, to work alongside design staff. The school had used (native speaker) instructors in modern languages on one-year appointments.

Sheila Galloway

Supply Cover Choices

Fieldwork included observation of the coordinator at work between 8.00 and 8.30 am. In her office on west site, she created the day's cover sheets, described by the principal as 'these infamous blue sheets'. Miss Brown had taught at Richardson School for thirteen years. As deputy in charge of INSET, she had found staff development vulnerable to lack of appropriate cover and re-organization of deputies' roles had combined the two areas with additional curricular responsibilities. Usually possibilities were pencilled in on the cover sheet from the previous day, where absence was foreseen, (scheduled training or because a teacher was already ill), but many mornings brought phone calls to announce short-notice absence.

The Employment Choice

This choice crystallizes in the decision to employ an external supply teacher. The first three days of illness were normally covered internally, but thereafter Carol Brown used external staff whenever possible. INSET was covered by supply teachers and agreed well ahead: she booked these sessions a half-term in advance. During her first year managing supply cover she had monitored cover lessons required of each teacher, but hospitalization and long-term illness, particularly at head of department and senior management level, had drained staff resources. Teachers interviewed recalled a sense of 'all hands to the pump'. During the summer some regular supply teachers found jobs, leaving Carol 'desperate' in September with only one supply teacher available, and a part-timer doing extra hours as supply. Already predictable absence for INSET was sending warning signs; 'Working half a term ahead I could see I was in trouble'. An advertisement in the local newspaper produced eighteen responses by letter or by phone, which she supplemented from the County supply list. She envisaged using these alongside the familiar people, and explained to those who responded to the advertisement:

> What I sometimes need is a group of teachers that I can call in for a specific day to let out a year team who could then have a workshop or a faculty team . . . but I couldn't always guarantee they'd get their own subject.

Nor could she guarantee staff that a subject specialist would cover their lessons. Equally, when external supply came to cover a specific teacher's

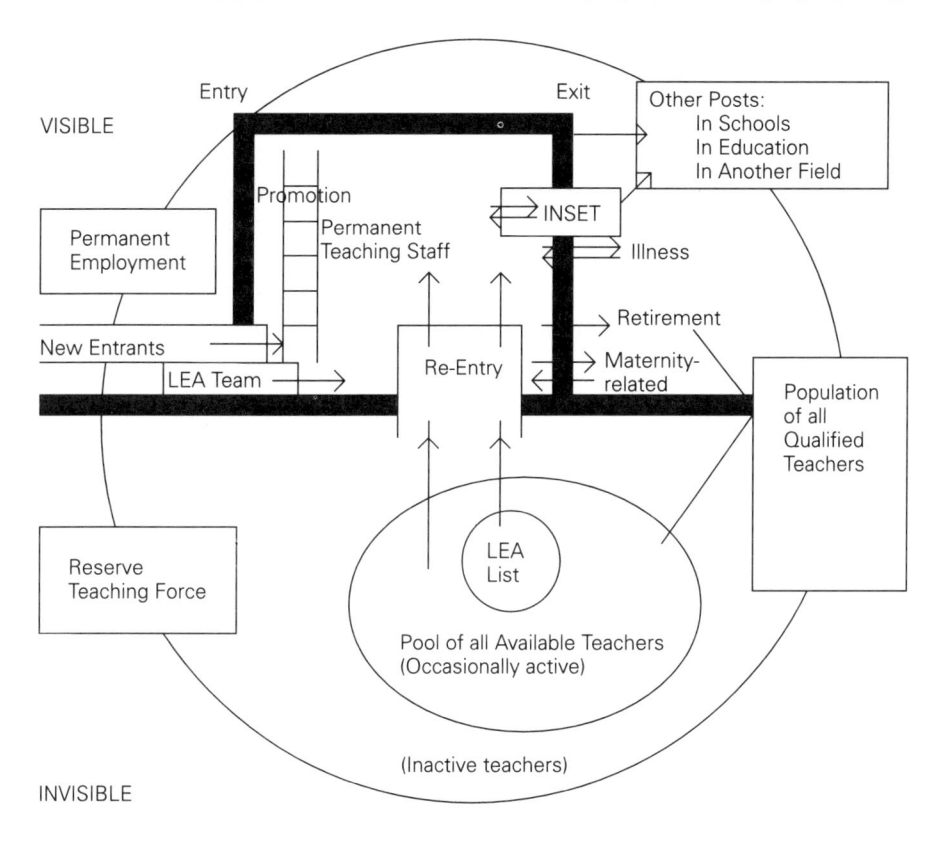

The Supply Coordinator's Role in Employing and Deploying Staff

Figure 1: School-supply Links

absence, no guarantee was given to allocate the individual to the foreseen absence: sometimes events meant it proved more effective to redeploy this person elsewhere and/or use internal substitutes. Appreciating the reasons for these moves she saw as a process of 'educating' staff. Carol Brown was hopeful about having more people to draw on during the coming winter, thanks to the advertisement:

> Now, the proof of the pudding is going to be when I need a team and I start to ring these people and they say, 'No, I can't come': that's a problem that you have, as to their availability, but, you know, that's something you can't know until the occasion arises.

The concepts of visibility and invisibility are central to the employment relationships that link supply teachers with schools schematically presented in Figure 1. As teachers in permanent employment move in and out of the school setting, their activities are essentially visible. However the pool of inactive teachers (in the past numbering around 400,000 qualified people) remains an invisible population (though numerically close to the total employed teaching force). A smaller number of individuals appear on LEA lists. The advertisement was a short-cut to make direct contact with this amorphous group especially those not yet on the County list. Using the local newspaper was a telling move, since many supply teachers on the County list lived at some distance. Miss Brown appreciated their reluctance to travel:

> Our afternoon is only an hour and three-quarters and they get paid hourly. So to come ... twenty-two miles and get paid an hour and three-quarters isn't very good ... That's why I tend to feel we need people who can just pop along.

The supply teacher moves briefly or sporadically from the invisible hemisphere of inactive teachers into the visible world of the employed. But without a contract of employment, leaving the premises means a return to invisibility, sometimes detectable in the language of teachers, as in one response to a question about procedures for supply staff following a day in school: 'I just assumed that they go to the car and disappear'. Even for a teacher who had herself done some supply work: 'Most of them come and go ... We find they are very anonymous'. Carol Brown had to cut through that anonymity. The advertisement was a formal way of doing this, and friendly, supportive contact, on the phone or face-to-face, maintained the personal relationship.

Educational Choices: Specialism and Continuity

The 'round holes' of staff absence are filled by 'pegs' of varying size and shape. The expertise of internal staff is assessed against the skills of supply teachers, and in the light of particular classes to be covered. A specialist supply teacher was engaged whenever possible, but unless they knew that a colleague from their department was scheduled to cover, teachers generally assumed that a substitute would not be a specialist, as did a head of department: 'the person who comes in will not actually be able to do more than be a sort of police body in the classroom'. Supply (or inactive) teachers with subject skills may not be prepared to take on what is asked. Carol Brown found it best not to pressurize even in extreme difficulty. Finding a qualified person was only the first step:

> It was obvious that she was reluctant and the more I pushed her the more excuses she came up with and so I backed off because I felt there was no point in pressurizing her to come . . . if even a little thing went wrong she was going to be so unhappy, that it wasn't worth the risk.

Teachers with general teaching skills were called on to cover in any area. The principal explained:

> Usually we're relying upon somebody who is a good disciplinarian, handler of a class, who we know will make sure that the work that was set is done . . .

There was value in having a confident teacher who knew school and pupils, was adaptable and resourceful, could relate to all age groups, and would tackle cover situations positively. If there were particular subject areas that she or he could not teach, in the sense of introducing new work or explaining important concepts, nevertheless such a person would maintain a class's momentum with set work. Secondary schools visited in this project welcomed supply teachers with such a profile. One 'generalist' at Richardson was Susan Bell, who is central to a later example.

Some areas of the secondary curriculum present specific problems. Craft, involving heavy equipment governed by safety regulations, is wholly vulnerable when the regular teacher is away. Lessons in cookery, games, or drama may be completely reorganized. Laboratory work may be postponed and a 'paper and pencil' exercise set. Practical music-making will not take place. Even a history teacher, 'wouldn't give group work to be done, I wouldn't give discussion work, I wouldn't give a video programme to watch'. Observation of both permanent and supply teachers supervising or teaching lessons showed that for both groups, there are times when specialism becomes an issue. Modern languages present a particular problem for the coordinator juggling pupils' needs against the skills available. With oral work now a major component of language teaching, students need competent input from a specialist and opportunities to communicate themselves. When teachers set work, as one language teacher commented:

> It's going to be very tedious work. It's all going to be writing which is not the usual pattern in language lessons.

'Setting work' for a planned absence could become a matter of saving written assignments or illustration work for the date in question, as with the RoA training:

> I do find this setting of work a real problem . . . I had to set work for the fourth year [year 10] low-ability group where we do virtually no writing . . . Setting work for that type of class is extremely difficult because nearly all the work I do is oral.

The head of sixth form had tried to support a lower-sixth group retaking GCSE English:

> I'd been in . . . once or twice just to see how they're getting on . . . and the subject isn't far away from my own specialism, but I can't help them. They're redoing some coursework and they need a specialist in there. Not only a specialist, but someone who understands the whole process of retaking.

Medium-term teacher absence can affect pupil motivation and progress. The French department had in the previous year rewritten timetables so that teachers took extra classes to ensure their progress, whilst other lessons were covered by non-specialist staff. One recalled:

> All of us took extra lessons last year: not cover lessons, proper teaching lessons, because we felt that the children were really suffering because cover in this case wasn't the answer.

They had later attempted to compensate by giving affected classes to teachers aware of their previous problem:

> I had them this year and I felt they have suffered because we had done some things extremely quickly . . . things were so fuzzy in their minds. I really had to concentrate on the essentials. We had no time for real practice.

Sometimes existing teachers have to take on extra classes, for instance, to protect examination groups. Sometimes non-specialist cover recompenses for some part of their overfull timetable. But this is at best a survival strategy, and raises issues of note, not just in terms of teachers' conditions of employment. Laudable attempts to protect one class can disadvantage others and pragmatic responses may mean disregarding other groups. A head of department described:

The Supply Coordinator's Role in Employing and Deploying Staff

> Making very arbitrary decisions and trying to . . . get the maximum teaching to the maximum number of pupils . . . and fairly callously having to push the bits that don't fit to one side for the moment.

Inevitably, spreading more widely the specialist skills of one teacher affects the time and energy available to other classes. (A primary parallel exists where a classteacher conducting SATs testing becomes ill, and a colleague who knows the children stands in. The second teacher's class has the supply teacher. The pragmatic solution protects the testing procedure but two classes are affected.) Where the need for specialist skills and knowledge is paramount individuals and institutions respond to events as best they can, sometimes making notable efforts to absorb the repercussions of teacher absence and protect high-priority groups. Supply coordinators can be generous in praise of staff rallying to limit the damage. In recognizing this, we should not dismiss 'knock-on' effects: the consequences of coping in this way may spread to other pupils even if the immediate problem is contained.

In seeking subject competence qualifications are not a certain safeguard. Surprises happen, as with the language specialist who proved to be 'three generations back in terms of technique'. Equally important is knowing the limits of one's own understanding and competence. Permanent colleagues were as likely as external supply teachers to overestimate their ability: one teacher recalled an

> absolute disaster . . . This is so embarrassing: one doesn't know how to put it to the children that all these phrases they've been given are totally incorrect and on no account should they use them.

This class had to be told, 'I'm sorry, we can't accept that'. The ideal for the modern language department was a former member of staff who began to do supply work; 'the difference between that and other supply teachers was vast'. Staff set work with confidence; the head of department noticed:

> She had the commitment to it . . . it was much more than just for the lesson. She went home one day sort of carting a pile of books because she was coming back the next day . . .

The case of modern languages at Richardson School demonstrates how specialist skills and knowledge are critical to pupil learning.

Examples from other schools and subjects parallel this case (e.g., Morrison, 1993). We must be glad for schools which resolve staffing problems with a committed supply teacher who marks work after school, but should we not also repeat earlier questions about the real interests of supply staff?

All supply coordinators attempt to protect continuity of teaching and learning, but the balance between specialist teaching and continuity is a fragile one. Another solution at Richardson was to split teacher contact with examination classes between members of a department and the supply teacher working with their support. Here the principle of continuity (of teacher) was tempered by the principle of guaranteeing quality of teaching.

Personnel Management Choices

Short-term decisions about deploying staff made in fleeting moments prior to the school day draw on physical as well as human resources. Transfer between sites was an ever-present issue. As in most split-site schools, Richardson staff absorb such trips into daily routine, but some lesson changes could be logistically awkward for anyone unfamiliar with the sites: newcomers needed to be quick off the mark when transferring. This affected Carol's decision-making in some but not all cases.

Schools develop supply cover systems that fit their aims and organization and are operated by senior staff with high profiles and a position of power in their schools. The nature of the supply coordinator's role is that it becomes one with the management style and personality of the individual. In interviews in a range of schools staff often spoke of the supply cover system in terms of the person responsible for it. The interpersonal skills required are many (Galloway, 1992b) and a guiding principle in Carol Brown's approach was updating her staff register with the running total of each teacher's cover lessons, to avoid inequalities and overloading. Cumulative effects could be assessed as the term progressed, so that her own sense of overall strain and stress was confirmed or refuted by this chart. If her feeling that staff were 'taking a bit of a hammering' was confirmed, then a borderline decision on engaging a supply teacher might be influenced: 'I've then sort of said to myself, "Well, really, I owe the staff a bit; things aren't going very well for them". So I'll buy in a day'. The chart's accuracy was essential, and she pointed to the page: 'You have to watch it carefully, hence the rubbings out'.

The Supply Coordinator's Role in Employing and Deploying Staff

At 8.25 am each day Miss Brown phoned a secretary on east site, dictating the cover sheet for the staff room notice board there. At west site, the staff briefing at 8.40 allowed her to convey information relating to cover. Here again, the style of delivery showed that their contribution in covering for colleagues was recognized.

Occasionally in any school lack of information, an emergency, misunderstanding or oversight leads to a class not having a teacher after the start of the lesson. Usual procedure is for a pupil to report this to the staffroom or school office; more often a member of staff will notice the omission before the lesson. When this happened, Carol Brown made it a personal request to a teacher to supervise the class, giving an assurance that this would be logged as a cover session. This need to be sensitive to individuals was noted in other schools. Staff morale is clearly linked to an awareness that the supply coordinator understands their position and that unreasonable demands are not made. (See Schoolteachers' Pay and Conditions Document, 1993). Miss Brown recalled relationships strained to breaking point during industrial action in the mid-1980s, and past disgruntlement when supply sheets had appeared to call unfairly on certain teachers. She strove to be fair and to be seen to be fair. This could further complicate decisions about cover but to maintain morale she fostered a climate where colleagues understood the situation and did not resent giving non-contact time:

> If I can reduce the aggro and get people to volunteer then they're going to do it with the right attitude and won't go along and say to the children, 'Well, I've been sent here and I don't want to be here — you get on', and then the children get the backlash.

The supply coordinator's day begins with an interplay of employment choices with the educational priorities of providing qualified teachers and maintaining continuity of learning. She had another aim:

> I want the children to feel that they're not missing out on too much.

Decisions may be partly shaped by school premises, and by personal and professional relationships, between teachers, (internal and external), and between the coordinator and other staff. To minimize resentment, Miss Brown would not pressurize teachers who were unwell:

> To me it's foolish economy to say, 'Can't you possibly come?'
> ... Because if you're not well and somebody is saying you've
> got to be here, that's not going to help you, is it?

Short-term decisions are enacted against a long-term background of school aims for the well-being and learning of pupils and staff, in the face of particular medium-term staffing situations. A philosophical approach is essential, and Carol Brown felt she was 'better this year than I was last year when I was new at it. I think you develop your own technique'.

The 'Proof of the Pudding'

Specialist Knowledge and Confidence

The first opportunity to field some of the new supply teachers was the RoA training. Releasing so many staff simultaneously was a novel event: nineteen staff would be away from classes at some point, though some only needed one lesson covered. A total of forty-one lessons (on a six-period day) required substitute teachers, the bulk of this being for RoA purposes. Miss Brown calculated the cost as £700. Eight supply staff were booked, of whom two were completely new to the school. Of these, Alex Gregory was allocated to technology and science because of his background. He began with two hours with year 7 technology, followed by one lesson with a year 11 group. During period 4 he taught science to year 10 pupils. After lunch he had another year 10 group, and the day would end with year 7 science.

Period 5 ran from 2.05 pm to 2.55. Mr Gregory found the right laboratory in the science block. In the corridors, pupils were waiting outside labs; it was a heavy afternoon and the corridors were not easy to negotiate while referring to room numbers. The weather had worsened during the lunch-hour, bringing some pupils indoors early into those buildings to which they had access. By three o'clock condensation would be running down the windows. Outside lab 4 a queue of year 10 pupils watched him approach.

Inside the laboratory, the twenty-eight members of this science group, girls and boys in equal numbers, are soon noisily settling stools at the benches. Alex Gregory checks the tray of equipment and lesson notes (which he has collected from the nearby technician's room). He allows the noise to continue until everyone appears to have a place, then, standing centrally in front of the board, introduces himself in a forceful voice which rises over the animated conversations:

The Supply Coordinator's Role in Employing and Deploying Staff

My name is Dr Gregory, and I'm here for this afternoon's session. I don't know what exactly happened to Mr Holt your regular teacher, but I'm sure we're going to be fine provided we do our work nicely and quietly and we don't waste time here and there . . .

He takes the opportunity as pupils settle down to glance through the material provided at the demonstration bench and voices the opinion that 'There are far, far too many in my opinion for a practical class'. This provokes some murmurs of discontent: he follows with 'I said, "in my opinion": I didn't say I was asking yours'. Glancing round apparently to assess the layout of the room, he cautions the group:

But for this reason I'm sure you will cooperate because if everyone says one word: louder, louder, and eventually we will get more noise and no work. So . . .

As year 10 subsides, he comments 'Excellent', (the first of several during the lesson). It is clear that imposing his mark on the session will not be altogether simple. The group seems well-disposed but has pupils who are already slow in settling down. Individuals appear helpful in finding equipment, but the noise level is not yet within a comfortable range, and he is still unsure about what exactly they are to do. Other features are to his advantage. Alex Gregory is more than average height, with a powerful voice and heavy (European) accent. This seems to intrigue some pupils (who later quiz him about his background). His manner in the classroom is to address the whole group in a quite formal way and then to go round, helping pupils working at each bench. Behind the strong voice and show of firmness, a hint of irony in his words and tone might mean that he would share a joke. But first he gets the lesson under way: books and worksheets are distributed, and he explains their task:

Mr Holt has prepared some work for you — some practical work to do. It concerns — I believe so far — something to do with onion, potato. [There are murmurs as pupils react to the information] I don't think we are frying anything . . .

What are the distinctive features of this session so far? Interviews with supply teachers indicate that classroom situations can leave them professionally exposed and vulnerable. They often work in isolation, with minimal guidance on lesson purpose and content, or the abilities of pupils. They need good classroom management skills, the ability to think on their feet, assess quickly the nature of an unfamiliar group, and speedily establish a working relationship with pupils. Earlier research (e.g., Loveys, 1988; Trotter and Wragg, 1990) identified the need for such skills, including an air of confidence (even if it is no more than that). Supply teaching can indeed be a risky business undertaken in unpredictable circumstances. Our research explored in different ways the extent to which supply teachers are visible or invisible. In the literature this invisibility has been identified (Galloway, 1993b). It features in school systems also. In interactions between individuals and groups, supply teachers frequently remain anonymous (see also Morrison, Chapter 4 in this volume). This discrepancy between high-profile, high-risk classroom teaching, and the inherent invisibility of the successful substitute is already evident in the opening minutes of Mr Gregory's lesson with this group.

Introducing himself by name in positive terms, including reference to his higher degree, is a bid for status and control. His opinion about the unsuitability of doing practical work with this size of class stamps him as an individual, outspoken, making professional judgments presumably based on experience. The reminder that their opinion has not been requested establishes what the pupil's relation is to be to the teacher, while voicing an assumption that all reasonable people will cooperate seems to imply recognition of a rational, mature approach. (Later he will use a different ploy to motivate a younger class, by comparing them with pupils at another secondary school where he most frequently does supply teaching.) The 'excellent' helps lighten the tone, as does the comment about the vegetables. His accent may, if anything, strengthen his position. Yet the opening uncertainty about the reason for Mr Holt's absence reveals, (as does the 'so far') the extent to which Alex Gregory is not yet fully conversant with the purpose of the lesson and the activity set.

If the personal introduction attempts to counter the image of anonymity, it is still a fact that he has not been in this school before. The relationship with this group will exist for less than an hour. As an understudy he has to help the action to proceed without imposing his own personality unnecessarily. Yet to establish control of the classroom situation with a lively group of pupils he must draw on personal resources and show individuality. One senior teacher conveyed graphically the pressure on supply staff to establish control in the classroom:

> It's the sort of job where you can sink before you've even had a chance to swim if you're not careful.

The Supply Coordinator's Role in Employing and Deploying Staff

Interviews with supply teachers revealed the tension associated with maintaining continuity for pupils by keeping a low profile, even adopting a bland manner, to minimize disturbance to the class's routine, yet simultaneously establishing one's standing in students' eyes as a capable teacher, which calls for a more assertive style. This divergent pull is an inherent feature of any experience as a substitute, whether the locum in the surgery, or the understudy on stage. Primary schools offer different but comparable examples of this tension.

Mr Gregory gives out worksheets and books. This is not wholly straightforward. Are books in a pile those that are normally used? He learns that they are not: 'Why do they supply me with these then?'. The pile of worksheets seems to be short:

> I'm not quite sure if we have enough copies so could you please just make sure you've got access to at least a piece of paper. If I give one to every two people for the time being ...

With the assignment before them, the class concentrates on the lesson's tasks. It is several minutes before Mr Gregory has time to read carefully through the full notes himself and absorb exactly what is required, and at this stage he does not attempt any sort of scientific explanation. Instead he focuses on the worksheet:

> Right. The procedure is simple. We simply work through the worksheet ... Anything that we need is either here [on the sheet] or within this room. If you're not quite happy or not quite sure, simply ask; if you do need any help ... just ask. I'm sure I don't have to repeat it as though you're first years. You've been here for how long? Four years now? So.

This strategy occupies the class while he familiarizes himself with the exercise, then moves around dealing with queries. He warns that the benches may need to be wiped before starting the practical work, and that if the notion of drawing to scale causes any problem, they should ask for help. A boy distributes exercise books. The exercise is to observe and sketch part of a potato and to test the potato and onion for starch using iodine. This seems to be within pupil capabilities, and most complete the work well before the end of the lesson.

I argued above that the educational choices made by the supply coordinator relate to specialism and continuity. From a new list of supply teachers Carol Brown had selected someone who understood science, was confident in laboratories and able to help pupils complete the work set by their regular teacher. Despite the prepared work (and equipment), operating in unfamiliar circumstances brought its own uncertainties. It would seem that Mr Gregory's priority in the first phase of the lesson was to establish himself. Initially he seems to give little attention to the scientific aims of the lesson. However, discussions with individuals reveal the levels at which pupils are working and problem areas so he draws the class together several times to explain particular points to the whole group. The specialist input increases as the lesson progresses. He clarifies the principle of scale drawings, and discusses the use of iodine to detect starch, evidently recapping what the class has learned previously. He counsels care when using scalpels to cut specimens, and since pupils have asked about the 'eyes' of the potato he explains their role in the development of the root system. Pupils contribute to these discussions, and he finds time to look through the unfamiliar text book, and advises them where this gives further information about vegetative reproduction. He moves from one group to another, covering all areas of the lab, and pupils also bring their work to him. The formal note of the early minutes is never completely regained.

The more scientific discussion does not reduce a need for quick responses. Pupils are working, but noisily: a persistent offender is asked, 'Every time I stop talking, why do you start? Surely you have all lunch to talk about the problems that you have . . .?'. Towards the end of the lesson, singling out one boy:

> Hey! Excuse me. There's an expression: 'Silence is golden', right? So let's keep quiet and make a little gold. Seriously now, because I have to explain some things individually . . .

He confiscates an item which one boy is fiddling with, and raises his voice to another who is distracting his near neighbours. One who has come inadequately prepared is told 'That's like telling me I forgot to get dressed this morning'. At 2.45 pm a sudden deluge of rain distracts by beating on the windows: he settles the class back to work. At 2.50 two pupils hand in books, decide that the lesson is over and put on anoraks: they have to remove them again. Remarks and actions are balanced by the occasional touch of irony; when it seems that there are insufficient specimens, for instance:

> Can I propose a solution please to the problem of the shortage of produce here? If you cannot find a potato could you just go to the next stage and study the onion first — OK?

The Supply Coordinator's Role in Employing and Deploying Staff

Later,

> When you have finished with your potatoes and onions and you have chopped them and made them into a thousand pieces as most of you did — you have mutilated my potatoes and onions — please could you bring them and put them into this bag here. Right. And don't forget . . . I don't have to tell you this, but: please wash your hands.

In the final minutes he conducts a brief résumé of what has been learned. When a boy responds 'We looked at onions and potatoes', he takes issue: 'That's what you *did*. What have you learned? If anything'. The message is repeated that potatoes contain starch; iodine enables us to test for starch, since it appears blue or even black depending on the concentration. When the bell goes, Mr Gregory is apologizing to the class: 'Sorry for calling you "ladies and gentlemen" — because I don't know your names'.

A non-specialist teacher might have taken this lesson, and supervised the use of scalpels and iodine. In other respects, however, the input that the class receives has the mark of someone confident in laboratories, concerned about detailed observation, at home with procedures of testing and recording. Though not apparent in the opening moments of the lesson, when the teacher has other priorities, these features later become evident. Doubtless, this lesson taught by Mr Holt would have differed from that observed. But Mr Holt was benefiting from training. Meanwhile, what took place in the science class was far from being 'childminding'. Virtually every teacher interviewed in this project made distinctions between supervising a class and engaging in an active teaching role. The example given here is of the latter.

Finally, in relation to teaching expertise, this teacher had come to this country only as an adult. He had advanced academic qualifications, but had not trained as a teacher. He had been approved some years before in another authority to do supply work and had worked since then on an occasional basis to supplement the business interests which were his prime concern.

Continuity

Previous sections showed why the supply coordinator employed an unfamiliar teacher, and gave a glimpse of how that decision presented in the classroom. However, the school often engaged more generalist teachers. Susan Bell had taught full-time at Richardson several years before and had done supply teaching since her children were young. In

Sheila Galloway

1991–2 she had a temporary contract for one afternoon weekly teaching games. For Carol Brown, sending Mrs Bell to a class was an option almost without risk. Her curricular strength was games but she would engage positively with any subject set at any level, apart perhaps from German. In action, she could be characterized as taking a facilitating role. Left to show a video to a year 8 history class, she coped with the machine, and led a useful discussion preparatory to the written work set for the lesson. As pupils worked, she covered every corner of the classroom, helping where asked.

With year 11 geography on GCSE assignments, she handled pupils as distinct individuals, again moving round the room for much of the lesson to look at their reports of individual projects. Her tactic was to discuss with them not as a geographer but as an interested adult. Themes centred on the immediate locality (river pollution, shopping patterns and local development), so her local knowledge and community involvement was relevant. Dialogues with individuals obliged them to articulate the purpose and method of their studies, and drew others into discussion. Some worked hard; others were usefully employed as long as they felt she was aware of them. A small number wasted time: her discussion with the two who had brought no work took the line that in wasting their own time they would face the consequences in the end. To reach this class in time she concluded the previous lesson at the west site very promptly and drove to the east site. Afterwards she described it as the sort of lesson that she most disliked because of some pupils' reluctance to work.

Year 9 pupils had just begun an English project on tourism. A worksheet spelt out tasks for the coming lessons and homeworks, but again, this was an active lesson. Mrs Bell used worksheet questions for discussion before pupils settled to writing. There was the buzz of working conversations, and again she circulated in the classroom as they worked.

If Alex Gregory felt the need to apologize for addressing pupils anonymously, Susan Bell had no such need. She knew pupils not just as a teacher, but as a voluntary helper at the junior school, from voluntary work with a youth organization, from having coached local children's sports teams, as a mother of three school-age children, and because she lived in the town. She used names and nicknames unselfconsciously, asked about sporting progress or families, and had a clear expectation of pupils. Many addressed her by name. These relationships helped in covering craft and design on the very day when a group decided their next option in the CDT activities rota. The system depended on students' guided choice, which had to cover a range of media and experiences. Susan drew here on pastoral rather than academic expertise, bringing her knowledge of some of the group to the session. When, as the end of school approached, most had made their choices and had no work or homework, she set pupils to plan how they might approach working on the new option. To a boy choosing metalwork who was lost for ideas, she described the gates of a nearby churchyard, suggesting he go and examine them over the weekend, as a start to his next project.

Such were the teaching situations that Mrs Bell encountered, and the classroom style she adopted, relying on an intelligent response to situations, engaging actively with pupils and subject matter, and transferring skills between curricular areas. It is clear why the supply coordinator often employed her. The ongoing relationship between school and supply teacher was long-standing. But there was no permanent contract, and no job security.

Finally, the supply teacher's dilemma about self-presentation was minimal in this case. Mrs Bell was far from being anonymous: known as a person and a teacher, she appeared at ease with the role and able to concentrate in the classroom on pupils and their work. The data suggest that her sense of identity derived as much from out-of-school as from professional activities. The strength lay in bringing from these life experiences what was of practical use to her as a supply teacher at Richardson School (Compare Chapters 4 and 12). More than any other supply teacher encountered, she found ways of bringing the 'invisible' world of non-employment into school.

We could draw conclusions from these examples in terms of the core and periphery model. We could explore the nature of real interests in this case and the power relationships operating. We could consider the data against notions of professional development or alternatively de-professionalization. We could use gender as a way of analysing the data (see Chapter 1). Instead this chapter has centred on the supply coordinator's role and what actually happens in classrooms, on teaching skills and the balance between specialist and general expertise. Such trade-offs between specialism and continuity face each supply coordinator operating within a structure that in any way approximates to the Richardson model.

Conclusion

This chapter has explored the role of the supply coordinator in terms of structural features at institutional level. Secondly, it traced micro-level responses to macro-level educational trends and initiatives. Particular aspects of the case study school have been noted that affect supply cover, and data relating to modern languages and to two supply teachers at work exemplify the nature and outcome of decisions made by the coordinator and others. It was suggested that the relationship between institution and individual is a mutually dependent one, with visible activities in schools relying as much upon the largely invisible skills of supply teachers as the latter are reliant on schools for work. Whether supply teachers' real interests are met is however questionable. The coordinator's role rests upon effective decisions on employment, educational and other managerial grounds, with prime concerns for quality of instruction and continuity making choices between specialist and generalist crucial.

Note

1   This chapter draws on work done as part of a project funded by The Leverhulme Trust entitled 'Supply Teaching in English Schools; an investigation of policy, processes and people'. This research involved Robert Burgess, Sheila Galloway and Marlene Morrison and was conducted at the Centre for Educational Development, Appraisal and Research at the University of Warwick during 1991 and 1992.

References

ATKINSON, J. (1984) *Flexibility, Uncertainty and Manpower Management*, Brighton, Institute of Manpower Studies.
BASSEY, M. (1981) 'Pedagogic Research: on the relative merits of search for generalisation and study of single events', in *Oxford Review of Education*, 7, 1, pp. 73–94.
BLACKBURNE, L., ARKIN, A. and HACKETT, G. (1989) 'Poorly paid and powerless,' in *Times Education Supplement*, 6 October.
BROWN, S. and EARLEY, P. (1990) *Enabling Teachers to Undertake Inservice Education and Training*, Slough, NEFR for the DES.
BURGESS, R., CONNOR, J., GALLOWAY, S., MORRISON, M. and NEWTON, M. (1993) *Implementing Teachers' In-Service Education and Training*, London, The Falmer Press.
CONNOR, J. (1993) 'INSET and the issue of disruption in secondary schools', in BURGESS, R.G., CONNOR, J., GALLOWAY, S., MORRISON, M. and NEWTON, M. *Implementing In-Service Education and Training*, London, The Falmer Press.

DEPARTMENT FOR EDUCATION (1993) *School Teachers Pay and Conditions Document*, July.
EARLEY, P. (1986) *Questions of Supply: An Exploratory Study of External Cover Arrangements*, Slough, NFER.
GALLOWAY, S. (1992b) 'Investigating the Irregular and the Unpredictable: reflections on research on supply teaching', Paper presented at the St Hilda's Ethnography Conference, University of Warwick, September.
GALLOWAY, S. (1993a) 'Being an Inset Co-ordinator', in BURGESS, R.G., CONNOR, J., GALLOWAY, S., MORRISON, M. and NEWTON M. *Implementing In-Service Education and Training*, London, The Falmer Press.
GALLOWAY, S. (1993b) 'Out of Sight, Out of Mind': A response to the literature on supply teaching', in *Educational Research*, 35, 2, pp. 159–69.
HUFFERDINE, J. (1992) 'Temporary Accommodations', in *Managing Schools Today*, 1, 8.
HULME (1993) 'Supply and Demand', in *The Teacher*, May/June pp. 12–14.
LEIGHTON, P. (1990) 'Codification, Classification and Prescription in Teachers' Contracts', in SARAN, R. and TRAFFORD, V. *Research in Education Management and Policy: Retrospect and Prospect*, London, The Falmer Press, pp. 129–34.
LOVEYS, M. (1988) 'Supplying the Demand? Contract, mobility, and institutional location in the changing world of the supply teacher', in OZGA, J. (Ed.) *School Work: Approaches to the Labour Process of Teaching*, Milton Keynes, Open University Press.
LUKES, S. (1974) *Power: A Radical View*, London, Macmillan.
MORRISON, M. (1993) 'Running for Cover: substitute teaching and the secondary curriculum', in *Curriculum*, 14, 2, pp. 125–139.
MORRISON, M. and GALLOWAY, S. (1993) 'Researching Moving Targets: using diaries to explore supply teachers' lives', Paper presented at the British Sociological Association Conference, University of Essex, 5–8 April to be published in the selection of conference papers.
SHILLING, C. (1991) 'Supply Teachers: working on the margins: A Review of the Literature', in *Educational Research*, 33, 1, Spring, pp. 3–11.
STENNING, R. (1990) 'School Staff Employment Trends in the Maintained Sector: some agendas for research', in SARAN, R. and TRAFFORD, V. (Eds) *Research in Education Management and Policy: Retrospect and Prospect*, London, The Falmer Press, pp. 171–7.
TROTTER, A. and WRAGG, E. (1990) 'A study of supply teachers' *Research Papers in Education*, 5, 3.

Chapter 7

Then and Now: Supply Teaching in the Infant School

Cynthia Knight

What happens when a headteacher faces the prospect of a school day with insufficient teaching staff to organize children's learning effectively? In this chapter the author's account of headship in an inner-city infants school suggests a range of answers based on personal reflection and ongoing experience. Considered alongside changing LEA/school relations which include school-managed budgets, the chapter also introduces new players to the supply story — the private staff agencies — and assesses their likely impact against the current backdrop of curricular and legislative change.

Setting the Scene

It is seven o'clock in the morning. The phone rings. A sense of foreboding has been justified. A member of staff is too ill to come to work. I have lots of decisions to make in a short space of time.

I am the headteacher of a medium-sized infant and nursery school with 310 pupils in inner-city Birmingham. My route to headship has been varied and interesting and has included life outside mainstream teaching as a peripatetic E2L teacher. I have been both an advisory teacher and a classroom-based educational researcher. Experience as an outsider and an insider has provided insights not only into the problematic aspects of supply teacher use but also to the potential for deployment in positive and creative ways.

As in many small primary schools the staffing structure at Clifton makes us very dependant on supply teachers. Currently, nine classes are staffed by nine teachers and this includes a teaching deputy. One absence involves the loss of more than 10 per cent of the teaching labour force and inevitably has a significant impact on the school. We

Then and Now: Supply Teaching in the Infant School

have a support teacher whose responsibilities are to teach those pupils whose English is not yet fluent. Her job description specifically excludes use as a supply teacher except in emergencies; if she is used in this way children who need her specialist skills are denied them. Given that my greatest concern is to minimize disruption to children's learning at a crucial time in their school life, what other options are open to me this morning?

First, I could take the class myself. This is an option forced upon many heads of small primary and infant schools either because their budget does not allow them to employ a supply teacher or because they are unable to find a suitable substitute teacher at short notice. For a primary head, there are positive advantages in taking a class. It gives an opportunity to get to know the children better and increases my knowledge about individual children's progress. It also improves awareness of the teacher's work-load and day-to-day problems with children, equipment, or the classroom. It keeps a head in touch with the heavy National Curriculum demands in teaching thirty very lively individuals. (Perhaps Secretaries of State and other senior figures in education should be required to serve some time on the supply list?)

Disadvantages are both apparent and non-trivial. In addition to the unpredictable demands upon head's time — children's illness, discipline issues, problems with the building, visitors without appointments — there are predictable and increasingly demanding and numerous tasks to be undertaken. These include curriculum development, staff appraisal, managing the budget, raising school funds, supervising students and work-experience pupils, and the important, if time consuming, task of supporting parents in the community in an increasingly hostile environment (75 per cent of the parents at Clifton are unemployed).

Second, I could split the class. This is an option taken with extreme reluctance first, because it puts extra pressure on already hard-pressed class teachers, and second, because it denies an already overly large class of children a carefully planned programme of learning activities, with inevitable effects on progress.

Third, I could ring for a supply teacher. There are at least as many decisions to be made again if I take this option as there are several sources of supply teacher at my disposal. These include:

- my own list of people who have been recommended by other teachers or who have contacted me directly;
- the LEA Staff Agency; or
- various private agencies.

109

My preferred option would be to employ someone from my list. They are all, so to speak, tried and tested. They know the school, its routines and ethos, and the special nature of our multi-ethnic community. The problem is that this is time-consuming and not much help in an emergency. I may have to spend some time on the phone until I find one of them available and time first thing in the morning is at a premium.

The LEA staff agency which opens at 8 am and has an ansaphone from 6 pm–8 am will not be open for business and even if I wait until I get to school it is unlikely they will be able to provide someone at such short notice. Although LEA-supported, this agency also charges fees for its services over and above the cost of the supply teacher (although these will fall the more the agency is used). The private agency will be operating early in the morning and will usually be able to find someone at short notice. Their charges will be higher but one phone call will at least end my initial problem.

These, then, are the sort of initial short-term decisions I have to take when a member of staff is ill. Of course the urgency of that decision is not uniform. Staff appreciate the problems created by last-minute notification of absence. Whenever possible they let me know the evening before. Sometimes they have gone home sick the previous day and this provides an early warning of the need for supply cover the next day.

Not all demands for supply teachers are short-term or unpredictable. Cover for INSET and internal school development can be organized in advance as can additional support for particular targeted purposes. Difficult though it may be for financial reasons (see below), longer term or planned absence is more predictable and manageable. However, even in these cases final decisions about who to employ and from which source will still depend on some of the factors already mentioned. These and others are now explored in more detail.

Financial Resourcing

Perhaps the first and most pressing factor will be the amount of money in the cover budget which ultimately determines the resources available. Clearly essential is the need to make the most effective use of the budget. Before LMS — that is before schools began to manage their own budgets — decisions were much simpler. In most cases the LEA set clear guidelines on the use of cover. For example, first-day cover would be done by the school and then the LEA would attempt to find cover for the second day. Headteachers had very little choice about who they were given, although the LEA would try to match the experience of the cover teacher with the age of the children in school. When the LEA was given funds for in-service training school-based demands for cover grew as increasing numbers of teachers were released during the day for training. This was a new phenomenon for most schools and teachers. Initially, central staffing agencies experienced difficulties in meeting this demand; children and supply teachers were not always well matched. On occasion cover for absent teachers was not provided even when a school was entitled. (The issue of matching is discussed in a later section.) Even for small primary schools important changes have taken place as a result of the local management of schools. Decisions about cover and overall staffing are possible at the micro level. Such changes have supposedly increased the power of schools to ensure quality and efficiency. Whether this will happen remains to be seen. What is not in doubt is that the new system has increased the autonomy of schools in the management of cover. As part of the school's budget a lump-sum allowance is now paid to cover the costs of replacing absent teachers. This should enable the headteacher to manage the cover budget more flexibly and perhaps, in the future, more creatively than has been possible in the past. This is, of course, easier for secondary schools and larger primary schools with larger cover budgets, but there still may be opportunities in smaller schools.

Small Schools

Consider, for example, the options for a primary school which is able to set aside £15,000 annually for cover. The most difficult and financially damaging form of absence is long-term absence. In any financial year it is very hard to estimate the amount of money which will be needed as a reserve to provide cover for this purpose. Before LMS, schools did not need to worry about this matter since the LEA provided cover. Now, if a member of staff is away for a prolonged period a school may be faced with a bill which can reduce the cover budget dramatically.

The problem is that this is unpredictable and difficult to insure against. As yet, insurance firms have not been able to offer schemes which are sufficiently financially attractive to be viable. As a result many smaller schools will rely on the cover budget, although it is doubtful whether this will be sufficient to cover a small school for long-term illness. This is an important issue which remains to be addressed at LEA levels, perhaps by creating their own insurance scheme.

If ignored the prospect is that governing bodies will need to take much greater account of health and absence records when they recruit new staff than has been the case in the past.

There are also some other compensations from the new arrangements. With the greater flexibility brought about by managing their own budgets schools lucky enough to experience no long-term absence can use surpluses in their cover budget to employ part-time teachers or support staff. The latter can serve many functions and increase the performance of the school. For example, part-time teachers may provide cover to allow the release of class teachers for curriculum development. They may work collaboratively alongside other teachers offering unique opportunities for collegiate planning and teaching.

Part-time teachers can also be used to cover short-term absence providing the absence coincides with the time allocated in school. On the surface this seems to be an ideal solution since cover is available almost immediately and the covering teacher will know the children and be familiar with the ethos and curriculum of the school. On the other hand this way of covering absence can disrupt children's learning. Planned collaborative activities may have to be cancelled as a result of staff absence, and staff may lose their non-contact time with the resulting loss of good will. In addition, the role may not provide job satisfaction for the part-time teacher if planned activities are disrupted. More seriously, the school will probably have offered a short-term contract to the part-time teacher because money in the cover budget may not be available the following year; this may lead to job insecurity and lack of attachment to the school, both of which are bound to undermine part-time commitment. Sometimes schools employ teachers on a termly basis so that they are not financially committed for a long period, perhaps to use up surplus cover money at the end of the financial year. In these circumstances, asking a temporary member of staff to cover absent colleagues may well be counter-productive for the school.

The better option for most short-term needs whether predictable or not is to use external cover more flexibly on a daily (or indeed weekly) basis. The advantages and disadvantages of this have already begun to be explored. No large financial commitment has to be made at any one time, and cover can be employed flexibly as and when necessary. With a more effective use of the cover budget, staff can be employed for a specific purpose (for example, during assessment periods). Many schools involved in Key Stage 1 assessment take on extra teachers during the Spring and Summer terms to support teachers undertaking SATS.

Then and Now: Supply Teaching in the Infant School

At Clifton School we have begun to use this budget to employ supply teachers with different and special skills for curriculum enrichment. In the past year children have had access to an artist who specializes in Islamic pattern (many of the children at school come from Moslem families). A potter has worked with children and staff to produce beautiful decorated tiles in clay. A puppeteer has covered many curriculum areas including art and design, speaking and listening, writing, reading, and science. All of these activities enrich the children's school experience, and increase their self-confidence and esteem.

The areas mentioned here do not exhaust the special skills available from supply teachers who may, for example, offer music, dance, history, geography, or design and technology. Indeed any subject which enhances children's access to the curriculum and also increases the class teacher's awareness of the subject are valuable, especially in small schools where the permanent staff's specialist skills inevitably leave large gaps to be covered. Of course some funds are already available for advisory work through government and LEA INSET funding, but this only provides minimum support for more highly focused whole-school development. Judicious use of the supply budget can plug some of the gaps.

There are quite fundamental implications here for staff agencies whether private or LEA organized. If these agencies can provide the kind of specialisms which have only previously been offered to secondary schools then this might enhance their appeal. Teachers who are keen to work in their own specialist area of interest, but do not want full-time employment, or who do not wish to work in the secondary sector, find a high level of job satisfaction by offering expertise to the primary sector. A register of teachers able to offer this kind of service would be invaluable.

Another option for small schools is to group together and share supply teachers. This might be particularly appropriate in a large authority like Birmingham where schools are located together in close proximity and hence this kind of arrangement is geographically viable. This already happens informally where a supply teacher is 'on the books' of several schools. However, a more formal financial link between schools is more complicated and may prove unworkable in these competitive times. (This issue is considered further in the next section.)

The management of the cover budget, therefore, is an increasingly important area of concern for headteachers and governors because it involves two very fundamental entitlements, namely access to the National Curriculum for pupils, and access to training for their teachers.

For schools with small budgets under LMS these entitlements are by no means automatic and it may be increasingly difficult for these schools to ensure that disruption to pupils' education does not occur when staff are ill. In addition, an increasingly heavy administrative role for the headteacher means that taking on the traditional role of 'extra supply teacher' may no longer be possible. Making the most effective use of resources may simply not be enough if overall resourcing is too tightly constrained.

Availability

Several sources of supply are available to schools. It has been school practice to build lists of teachers willing to do supply work. This system can work well. Supply teachers get to know schools, children, and routines. Headteachers select teachers who seem to fit in with the school and are known to be reliable. For various reasons, however, supply teachers come and go. Good mature returners who want permanent jobs find them. Supply teaching is a good way of advertising your talents and gives the teacher the chance to sample the school on a day-to-day basis. Accepting a permanent job offer is less of a gamble; not surprisingly, supply teaching is an attractive way back, notably for the female teacher who has chosen to take time out for child rearing. Older teachers retire, and so their availability is constantly changing. Also good supply teachers are probably on the lists of several schools, and so are not always available. The system, then, is by no means infallible, and cannot be relied upon as the sole source of supply staff.

In Birmingham LEA the Central Supply Agency was traditionally almost the only source of long and short-term cover. For various reasons it was put under great pressure when the demands on it grew as a result of government grants for in-service training which allowed teachers to train during the working week. This was a new phenomenon for classroom teachers and the central agency found it difficult to cope. Headteachers became increasingly irritated by the failure of the Central Supply Agency always to meet the demands placed upon it. Sometimes cover staff did not appear, or the supply teacher's experience did not always match children's needs. As heads began to manage their own budgets and were more able to decide when they employed a supply teacher they felt that they needed, (and were entitled to) a service which would respond quickly and efficiently to the demands made on it. At this time also, schools with delegated budgets had a lot more freedom to manage their own cover budgets.

As a result the monopoly of the LEA supply team loosened and private agencies were set up. Currently, Birmingham has at least three private sources of cover. Since these are a relatively new phenomenon it is difficult to assess their quality in any systematic way. However, it has generally been the experience of schools using them that they try to be responsive to needs. Often on call for long periods of the day and at weekends, they are very rarely unable to provide cover, even on an emergency basis. At present they are more costly than the LEA staff agency but it seems likely that in order to provide a more flexible service in future, the LEA staff agency will also have to increase its charges and undergo some re-organization (see below).

Quality

If minimizing disruption to pupils' learning is the primary objective in the ideal supply situation, the quality of replacement teaching and learning is crucial when headteachers or senior managers make decisions about whom they employ, even though in practice availability may be the initial primary concern.

Supply teachers come in all shapes and sizes. Among the more interesting have been an artist specializing in Islamic pattern and teaching part-time at the Victoria and Albert Museum, a young man on a bike who brought as preparation for thirty lively 7-year-olds some card and rubber bands (we never really found out what he did with these), several very lively overseas teachers (especially from Australasia) whose enthusiasm and knowledge of their home countries helped us cover many attainment targets in geography, and several travellers who paid for their exciting trips by teaching in the summer and then escaping to warmer climes during the winter. Categorizing our supply staff is not an easy task. In contrast, Earley (1986) describes four main categories: married women many of whom desire to re-enter teaching after a career break to have children; retired teachers prepared to help out now and again providing there was no adverse effect on pension rights; unemployed teachers for whom supply teaching was a useful means of by-passing ringfence policies and gaining full-time employment; and those for whom supply teaching fitted in well with their lifestyle (for example, actors, musicians, part-time researchers, and so on). Supply teaching was most suitable for those who wished to re-enter teaching gradually or augment other sources of income. For those with responsibilities for children supply teaching was ideal as it enabled family commitments to take precedence over professional ones.

From these groups it is important to get the best. How then are we to define quality? The temptation always is to invite back the teacher who can control the few 'difficult children' in each class since that causes the least extra trouble to the head and deputy. We may also be tempted to congratulate those who come armed with a sheaf of worksheets to keep the children quiet for the day. But are these teachers really contributing to the learning of the children or are they simply successful child-minders? Perhaps this is all that can be expected when teachers move quickly from one school to another. Often, supply teachers do not have regular training, particularly those who are not members of a permanent supply team. The rapidity with which the curriculum is changing particularly in primary schools, means that it is especially difficult for teachers who are not school-based to keep in touch with current practice.

This is clearly not a satisfactory state of affairs especially in inner-city schools where understanding about the uniqueness of children's bilingual abilities and the languages spoken are essential in order to get the best out of children. Such knowledge can be gained only by careful training or continuous experience in similar schools. Schools who now control their budgets and are constantly being reminded of their responsibility to monitor quality need to demand high-quality supply teachers.

Quality in supply teaching may not necessarily be the same as in permanent class teaching. A teacher taking a class for the first time will not necessarily be able to provide the differentiated activities expected of regular class teachers. However, this does not mean that the children are not provided with quality learning experiences which are also enjoyable. A very successful supply teacher recently made biscuits with a whole class at Clifton School. This required a great deal of good planning and organization but she will certainly be invited back, especially by the children. In order to achieve this it is essential either that the teacher has experience in teaching specific age groups or, if they do not possess that experience, realize that they need to be adaptable. The fallacious assumption, derived from a childminding view of supply teaching, that secondary or even junior teachers will be able to adjust their teaching style for infants has been the weakness of many agency staff. An ideal situation would be supply staff experienced in several phases but regrettably these are few and far between. The crucial requirement is the ability to adapt one's methods to the needs of each class and its pupils. In my experience young children, and particularly those who may be experiencing difficulty in the home, will find it difficult to adjust to their own class teacher's absence. Infant teachers are especially sensitive to this fact, but there is nothing to prevent a teacher with a 'top-down' approach to class management from acquiring the same awareness. A sensitive, caring attitude towards pupils and a willingness to learn are the valuable if not indispensable assets required.

In addition, if temporary staff are being paid at a similar rate to permanent teachers managers might presumably expect those teachers to be familiar with the National Curriculum, at least in the core areas. Commitment to, and an understanding of, equal opportunity issues are also essential for all staff teaching in Britain today.

A willingness to participate in school and children's activities especially when they relate to the regular teacher's programme is also desirable. Certainly supply teachers should be available for duties expected of regular teachers, for example, playground and dinner duty, where this is appropriate. Where teachers are employed over a longer period then the expectation should be that they participate in all activities including staff meetings and INSET activities. A certain amount of antipathy can develop towards supply staff when there is unwillingness to take part in whole-school activities.

Agencies

Although defining the ideal supply teacher is a relatively simple matter, ensuring that schools have access to quality substitute teachers is not. It is certainly a concern which the agencies, private and LEA, seem to be trying to address perhaps in response to school demands increasingly linked to budgetary control and 'value for money' issues.

The staff agency of the Birmingham LEA, for example, has recently prepared a three-way charter, or contract, which aims to provide a basis for improving links between schools, agency staff and agency line management. The document clarifies the roles, responsibilities and expectations of each of the three groups in relation to each other.

Strategies to provide professional and career development for agency staff are also now in place and no doubt this will serve to increase the adaptability of supply staff. For example, a new category of 'associate teacher' has been defined. These teachers will receive appropriate National Curriculum training and access to relevant phase expertise. Each associate will be linked to a particular geographical area enabling them to build up greater in-depth knowledge of individual schools. The issue of 'match' is also being tackled by using a selection process which is intended to fulfil the needs of schools more accurately. Of course, all these moves to provide a quality service will be under threat as the LEA is forced to delegate an increasing amount of the central training budget to schools who cannot provide the kind of training required by the central supply staff.

An interesting development has been the entry of recruitment agencies into the supply teaching market. Some agencies are operating solely as providers of supply teachers. They are usually run by people with previous teaching and/or educational management backgrounds. In addition, agencies with more general experience in labour recruitment are entering the market. One such agency has been established in Birmingham. In its advertising material it sets out to 'offer schools the most complete specialist and cost effective service available anywhere'. Apart from offering a twenty-four-hour service it also lays great stress on providing a highly personalized service.

> We will send one of our highly experienced education coordinators to visit your school. They will study your school's culture, personality and working practices whilst assessing your precise teaching requirements. From that assessment we will select the most appropriate teacher from our bank of available candidates to fill your vacancy. The recommended teacher will already have completed a medical history declaration and been thoroughly referenced.
>
> As standard we always check against the following criteria:
>
> - QTS check;
> - List 99 check; and
> - Criminal conviction check.
>
> The recommended teacher will additionally have been checked for their compatibility to the specifics of your brief namely:
>
> - necessary skills and experience;
> - attitude and suitability for your particular school;
> - reliability and flexibility; and
> - social adaptability.
>
> Following the teacher's placement one of our specialist account managers will liaise with you to monitor performance and to ensure that the required standards of teaching, productivity,

efficiency, behaviour and security are maintained for the duration of the booking.

In terms of its aims the above would seem hard to fault and could provide a useful model for other agencies. As yet, we have no evidence whether this particular agency can meet the high standards it sets itself. Availability of suitable staff at very short notice would seem to be an inevitable problem. The advertising material makes no mention of training or career development for its temporary staff, nor of issues like familiarity with the National Curriculum. These are issues that will need to be addressed if the service is to be satisfactory in the long term. In contrast with these potential areas of weakness the agency is firmly committed to equal opportunities and provides a strong policy in this regard.

Conclusion

One of the greatest difficulties in building up a source of highly qualified skilled and motivated supply teachers has been the way in which schools view supply teaching. Historically, and for various reasons, supply teachers have been viewed with a certain degree of suspicion, as, indeed, are all outsiders, including advisory teachers employed by the same educational authority.

The issue of the image of supply teachers is taken up in another chapter, but schools need to reflect on the ways they view supply teachers. Having spent time on the 'outside' I feel that opportunities to visit many schools, to observe 'good' and 'bad' practice, and to experience many different ways of teaching and school management, was an essential part of my preparation for senior management. Experience has shown me that schools and LEAs need to appreciate that effectively used and properly trained supply teachers can be enormously beneficial. Carelessly used and poorly trained they can be the opposite. Schools can do their bit by ensuring that supply teachers are welcomed as professionals and supported during their time with them, but the main responsibility for change lies elsewhere. LEAs could provide more professional development opportunities and emphasize their availability when recruiting staff. Secondments for permanent staff wishing to observe other schools, or even have a change of scene, could be offered more systematically than at present. Supply teaching is an excellent way for mature returners to have 'on the job (re)training' and indeed prepare for more senior posts but this needs the kind of resourcing which only LEAs or the Department for Education can provide.

Some LEA staff agencies are becoming more pro-active, by finding out about the needs of individual schools, and by providing a more responsive and high-quality service. This ought to be the pattern for all. Because of their greater capacity to provide coherent and effective training for supply staff they are uniquely placed. The most urgent need is for LEAs to protect the interests of heads, teachers and children in small primary schools who find themselves financially crippled by long-term staff absence and who, as a result, will not be able to provide adequate education for either their children or their teachers. An authority-wide insurance scheme to protect against these eventualities would seem the obvious solution and would make a little less traumatic those early-morning decisions, which headteachers of the smaller primary school so frequently face.

References

EARLEY, P. (1986) *Questions of Supply: An Exploratory Study of External Cover Arrangements*, Slough, NFER.

Part 3

The Employer in Different Guises

Chapter 8

Human Resource Management: An LEA Response

Pauline Buzzing

This chapter describes how West Sussex LEA established an authority-led initiative to encourage out-of-service teachers back into the classroom. In a region where alternative jobs were available, teacher-retention purposes were foremost: inactive teachers had to be encouraged to remain in the profession when other opportunities were open to them, and career break teachers were encouraged to return to work as soon as possible. Along with other contributions, the author reflects a transitional role for employers, in this case the local education authority, with consequences for supply teachers in this LEA and elsewhere.

LEAs are concerned to see that the best possible quality of education is offered to pupils in maintained schools. Bearing in mind levels of in-service training, sickness and other essential absences by school staff, this oversight involves some sort of quality control of supply teachers as well as of regularly employed teachers. This chapter focuses on West Sussex, an LEA which has played a role in disseminating good practice and in spreading information. It has provided for schools a short-cut to improvement through meetings, working parties and the publishing of documents. Headteachers meeting in family groups, in clusters; area meetings, whole-County meetings on the basis of age range, type of school or topics of current interest — all these provide a series of forums, networks and communications systems which are used for the spread of good practice.

West Sussex is a shire County on the south coast of England. It stretches from the Hampshire border in the west to the border with East Sussex on the outskirts of Brighton. The population is heaviest on the coast where the seaside towns of Bognor Regis, Littlehampton,

Worthing and Shoreham are. Inland are small market towns with some larger settlements like Burgess Hill, Haywards Heath and Horsham along the routes of the railway lines to London. In the north of the county is the post-war town of Crawley and the extreme north-eastern boundary just takes in the town of East Grinstead. The County town is Chichester in the south-west, eight miles from the Hampshire border. The rest of the county is rural.

The supply teacher system in West Sussex is operated on an area basis with lists circulated from the four area offices. Potential supply teachers complete a form which asks for details of education and training, work experience, personal details and names of referees. In many ways this application process is similar to that which any LEA uses with any applicant for a post. The requirements are that someone should have qualified teacher status in this country; that they should live within striking distance of West Sussex schools and that they should be able to provide evidence of recent successful teaching in a maintained school. Basic details are then circulated to the authority's schools enabling individual schools to get in touch with supply teachers as appropriate. This simple system has been used by many LEAs over a period of time. In recent years, however, it has been under pressure in a variety of ways. The strains have been created by teacher shortages and mismatches, by the pace of educational change and by local management of schools.

Teacher Shortages and Mismatches

Since the last war there has always been a pool of qualified teachers not currently teaching full-time who could fill in at short notice if needed. The size of the pool fluctuates according to the general employment situation in teaching which, in turn, often reflects wider economic trends. In the recession of the early 1980s competition for teaching posts was fierce. Reports of over 100 applicants applying for a single teaching post were not uncommon. Schools had plenty of choice, not only for full- and part-time posts but there were many teachers waiting to return who were more than willing to take up supply teacher vacancies.

Within five years the situation was showing signs of change. The birth rate had begun to rise in 1980 and this resulted in growing numbers in the primary schools from 1985. With the end of the recession industry began to flourish and to take many of our teachers away. Vacancies increased and the pool of non-teaching teachers became much

Pauline Buzzing

smaller. At the same time the pace of educational change was quickening. The Technical and Vocational Education Initiative (TVEI), funded by the then Manpower Services Commission, offered in-service training coupled with grants to enable daytime teacher release. This put pressure on secondary schools to find additional supply teachers. Previously, the balance between supply and demand had worked well, but this additional requirement strained the system. It was further complicated by in-service training for the new GCSE examination and, in the Spring term of 1986, it was clear that schools were experiencing extreme difficulties in finding enough supply teachers to allow teacher release for the training.

West Sussex's response was to set up the first LEA career break scheme for teachers. It began as a local initiative in the western area of the County with the specific brief of providing support for returning secondary teachers to see whether they might be persuaded to return a little earlier or to put themselves forward for supply teaching if their confidence could be built up and if they were abreast of current developments. It was agreed that, although the focus of the scheme was secondary teachers, primary teachers who came forward would not be turned away.

It seems surprising that support had not previously been offered but a quick look at DES regulations explains why this was so. Money for in-service training was strictly for employed teachers. It could not be used for those who were not employees of the LEA and the employment of supply teachers on a casual basis was not sufficient to qualify for the funding. The Manpower Services Commission funded the first two terms of the Keeping in Touch With Teaching scheme (KIT) and, by the time it had proved its effectiveness in a very dramatic way, the regulations had been changed so that funding could be used for any teacher who had qualified teacher status.

The form of support given to career break teachers through KIT is now well-known (Buzzing, 1989). KIT became the model on which many LEAs, large and small, urban and rural, based their supply, career break and returner training schemes. It was so successful because it was, and is, so simple and it had considerable impact on the numbers and on the quality of the supply teaching force in the county.

Investigations into the kind of teacher who joined KIT in the early days of the scheme revealed some interesting facts. First, they showed the impossibility of making too many generalizations about KIT members' experience, the length of their break and their areas of expertise. Second was the variation in their future aspirations in the profession. Both factors had an effect on the kind of scheme which emerged. The variation in their experience demanded a system of record-keeping, of good storage and retrieval systems where the information could be accessed. The length of the break had implications for levels of confidence, for the need for updating and for contact with the classroom. The wide range of areas of expertise meant a need for many different kinds of support and networks with advisory teachers, schools and the West Sussex advisers.

The variation in future aspirations meant adopting a flexible approach. Some KIT members saw supply teaching as a first step towards an eventual return to the profession. Others thought it unlikely that they would ever return to the classroom on a full or part-time basis. They liked the flexibility of being able to work when needed and of fitting in the demands of (mainly) family life with an employment commitment. They mentioned the ability to cope with sick children, to attend functions at their children's schools, of dovetailing paid work as one element in their portfolio with family commitments, social work in the community, hobbies and interests.

Yet others saw supply teaching as a long-term way forward because of the demands of partners' jobs. Frequent long absences demanded by some firms left women with a heavy burden of domestic responsibility which nevertheless fluctuated. Changing demands were also quoted by women who looked after elderly relatives who suffered bouts of illness and whose children suffered from conditions such as asthma where they felt unable to commit themselves to regular work. It was important to cater for both these groups in the scheme; for those who saw supply teaching as a stepping stone and for those who wanted to develop it as their permanent way of work.

The central core of the scheme — a newsletter and regular, local monthly meetings — was supported by a menu of other activities. Flexibility was important because the shortage of supply teachers was never uniform. It reflected for instance shortages within schools: modern languages and science heading the list for secondary schools and early years' teachers in the primary phase. These problems were relatively easy to address: modern languages and science groups were set up, meeting several times a term with a subject expert who had been a successful classroom teacher. Activities ranged from practical classroom experience to sessions on new materials and resources. Extra encouragement for teachers in shortage areas resulted in growing numbers of supply teachers and in good relationships with schools.

This was particularly important in the secondary sector where confidence needs to be at a very high level in order to encourage returners to come back to the profession. Secondary schools are large, busy and can be quite impersonal and very bewildering. One successful model was where a head of modern languages arranged a tea party for potential supply teachers in his area. He chose the time carefully to allow children to be collected from schools and provided activities for them. Then he and his staff sat down and talked with (rather than to) the half dozen potential modern languages supply teachers who came. They talked about the kind of support the department could provide; they offered opportunities for work shadowing and they built good relationships so that the supply teachers felt they would be working somewhere where they would be known and valued.

Primary refresher courses were run by the LEA with an emphasis on the early years and headteachers were heavily involved in the planning and delivery of these courses. It was clear that an improvement in the position of the supply teacher, and hence in numbers and quality, could not come about through the efforts of the LEA alone: the schools had an important part to play. Some had to make special efforts because of their geographical position. In this rural County the small primary schools were experiencing particular difficulty in finding supply teachers, Rates of pay for supply teachers had never been high and increasing fuel costs meant that teachers were reluctant to drive long distances to unknown schools. The small schools in one particular area decided to adopt a pro-active approach to recruiting supply teachers. They felt they had strengths to offer potential returners and supply teachers who lacked confidence: they could provide a welcoming environment and their small size meant it would be relatively easy to absorb the ethos of the school. They aimed to take the fear out of the supply teaching experience in order to make it as positive and productive as possible. The teacher recruitment base set about helping to make this a reality.

Heads agreed to fill in a form with basic information for the supply teacher — times of the school day; arrangements for wet play; contact names and telephone numbers; the number of classes in the schools and any special information, down to such basic details as a map showing the whereabouts of the school and details of where to park. Seventeen schools were involved and the sheets were collected inside a folder together with an introductory booklet. This contained information on how to organize life as a supply teacher: what to have in your emergency supply teacher kit and addresses and telephone numbers of professional and resource centres in the area. There was also a section on claim forms explaining how to fill them in and detailing the most common mistakes people made in filling in their form. The folders were then distributed freely to schools and to potential supply teachers alike and a series of training days was run to raise awareness of the benefits rural schools could offer.

Other schools needed to change because their policy toward supply teachers did not match their practice. On paper they were committed to providing the best quality of education for their pupils and their intention was to support and to sustain supply teachers who came to work in the school. The reality was quite different. Schools are busy places and supply teachers sometimes found themselves feeling unwelcome, without the right information about pupils they were teaching and with little knowledge of where equipment and materials could be found.

When KIT first became involved, surprisingly little information was available in most schools for their supply teachers. That which was provided ranged from very little to a secondary school handbook of 120 pages. What was needed was a booklet specifically designed for the needs of supply teachers with information extracted from the mass of the staff handbook. In the case of some primary schools the information would fit onto one A4 sheet. This apparent neglect was unintentional. The demands placed on schools have increased in recent years. Furthermore, the very times when supply teachers are in schools are those when the children are on site: the most pressured times of the day, when the focus of attention is (quite rightly) the young people. Sadly, the result of neglected adult/adult relationships acts adversely on the supply teacher situation and has a knock-on effect on the education of the pupils.

In some schools it had resulted in a culture of double standards where two levels of behaviour and work were tolerated — even accepted as 'natural'. Supply teachers were blamed for poor behaviour and, even if they were only in the school for a day, any disruption, perhaps for the rest of the week, was referred back to the effects of the supply teacher. This double standard extended to the kind of support the supply teacher might be offered. Some supply teachers told of staff going off with keys so that practical work set could not be completed; of access to school-stock cupboards being refused; of lack of information such as the whereabouts of another member of staff they could contact and of unwelcoming attitudes in staff rooms.

Most tellingly, pupils' work produced when supply teachers were in school was often treated with suspicion by other teachers. One supply teacher was told to set the children 'anything binnable' and it is not uncommon even today for work for the supply teacher to be done on paper and not to be allowed in the pupils' regular books. This lack of support on the part of a school sends messages to the pupils about the value and status of the person who is standing in for their regular teacher.

Such cultures do not happen by edict: they grow slowly and the LEA, at greater distance, could take a more detached view and suggest how schools could improve the way in which they treated their supply teachers who would then be given the chance to perform more competently and confidently. The upward spiral thus created would be of benefit to the pupils. Where supply teachers had information such as the names of other teachers, the routine of the school day, a plan of the school and information on the whereabouts of resources, the result was greater efficiency and confidence. The dissemination of good practice and information to schools, information sheets and supply teacher booklets resulted in an increase in the number and in the quality of supply teachers.

The Pace of Educational Change

Supply teachers have to cope with a wide variety of situations which may not have been part of their previous experience for the education system of England and Wales has always been characterized by variety. There are selective and non-selective schools; single-sex schools and mixed schools; schools which stream and schools which set and schools where mixed ability teaching is the norm. There are vertically grouped classes; village schools where the entire school may be in two or three classes; schools which work through topics and schools which operate an integrated day. In West Sussex many of these variations can be found within a single LEA.

Coping flexibly with this diversity is an essential part of supply teachers' skills but they must develop it for themselves, since initial teacher training offers no preparation for working as a supply teacher, despite the fact that many teachers will have a period of supply teaching in their careers. The skills are different from those demanded of a teacher who has classes or a class regularly on a full- or part-time basis. It requires a high degree of expertise and adaptability but, until recently, little help, advice or training was provided.

In the 1970s with little help or support supply staff coped with the new open-plan schools; they dealt with the comprehensivization of schools and they managed to deal with the move towards mixed-ability classes and away from single-sex schools. They were not part of the training programme for CSE yet they adapted and many continued teaching.

Human Resource Management: An LEA Response

When the pace of educational change began to quicken in the 1980s this provided supply teachers with a different challenge. No longer were the changes they were dealing with of an organizational nature: they were embedded in the curriculum itself. Further, the increased pressure on schools meant that they began to make different demands. It was not enough for the supply teacher in a primary school to come in for a day and keep the children busily and purposefully occupied. Time pressures demanded a greater concentration on continuity and on the National Curriculum.

The pace of change had three major effects on supply teaching which the KIT scheme tried to address. First it diminished confidence in supply teachers themselves who felt nothing was the same as it had been before they took a break. Second, it produced confusion in the schools as to what they were demanding of their supply teachers and third, they were left out of training altogether.

First, confidence in supply teachers ebbed. Building confidence is a slow process. Self-esteem tends to be low in our culture in general and it is a particular problem for women who are not encouraged to be assertive. For teachers, too, self-esteem is a problem. Research conducted as long ago as 1962 showed that teachers felt that the rest of society had a poor view of the profession Anonymous (1989). As 98 per cent of supply teachers are female, it is hardly surprising that their self-esteem should be particularly low and when that is related to particular situations such as coping with a group of pupils who may dislike the break in routine caused by the absence of their regular teacher, lack of confidence increases (Chessum, 1989).

Through the KIT scheme's investigations it also became clear that feedback systems for supply teachers in schools were often nonexistent. The supply teacher was expected to understand that if she or he was invited back to a particular school that was an indication that previous performance had been satisfactory. Rarely did heads or teachers comment on their perspective of how the day or days had gone. If the supply teacher's performance had been negative, the head was likely simply to remove that particular supply teacher's name from the list of teachers used by the school. In extreme cases this might also include a telephone call to the area office and in one case the supply teacher's name was removed from the lists for the following term without being told that this was about to be done.

In some schools, however, feedback was well done and headteachers or heads of department asked to see the supply teacher at the end of the day simply to exchange a few words and to build the relationship though a professional dialogue. Through KIT we worked on this from both ends, passing this on at heads' meetings and through booklets as an appropriate and helpful strategy and encouraging supply teachers to take the bull by the horns and to ask for feedback, even if none were offered.

Sessions on self-esteem formed part of the regular KIT meetings each term. Producing skills' inventories was salutary. Many supply teachers found it difficult to identify their own skills. Verbalizing them to a colleague was hard enough. Writing them down was even harder but was an important stage in acknowledging their existence. Having produced a list on paper, categorizing them provided another stage in the process and it also enabled returners to make broader statements about their abilities. If it seemed as though several of the skills listed involved interacting with others, the teacher was encouraged to add interpersonal skills to the list. So the question 'What are your strengths?' might be answered 'I'm very good with people' and the interview with the headteacher would be preceded by the supply teacher visualizing a positive outcome and including affirmations in her self-talk such as 'I handle situations with other people easily and effectively'.

This in turn led to a series of meetings where supply teachers were encouraged to go out and to market themselves. One of the problems encountered by supply teachers who had newly joined the list was that schools had a regular list of supply teachers whom they always used and it was difficult to break into the system. Individuals found that it was relatively easy to get onto the LEA list, but it was much harder to persuade a school to use them. Through KIT supply teachers were able to work on marketing strategies in a positive way and to develop good relationships with a number of schools. Thus the raising of self-esteem and the development of confidence in dealing with headteachers and heads of department formed part of the LEA's activities in the supply teacher field.

However, professional confidence in supply teaching rests firmly on a clear understanding of what is required and on feelings of professional competence and a second result of the quickening pace of change was the feeling that schools were no longer certain what they wanted from the supply teacher. To a certain extent, this confusion had always existed within and between schools. Some schools saw the supply teacher role simply as 'baby sitting' — a containment role which had to do with control and amusement rather than education and challenge. Others expected the supply teacher to produce continuity of learning, taking up the baton from the teacher who was absent and returning it after the absence was over.

The differences between primary and secondary supply work

provided even more distinctions: primary supply teachers expected, on the whole, that they would take work in with them whereas secondary teachers usually had to supervise work which had been set by the regular teacher, motivating, encouraging and supporting pupils often in subject areas which were not their own.

Further differences were found between long and short-term supply work. Supply teachers might find themselves covering absences of only a day — planned as in the case of in-service training or hospital appointments — or unplanned as in the case of sickness or accident. On the other hand, they might find themselves employed for two or three days, a week or a whole term. Sometimes it would be known that an absence was for a fixed time: in other cases an initial one day might turn into three or a one-week absence might stretch into two. How was training to be organized so that supply teachers could feel competent to cope with the demands of different schools in different situations with different requirements?

The answer was to run a range of courses for different purposes. Supply teacher support meetings were established and formed a regular part of the termly KIT programme. These had a wide focus: primary and secondary; potential and actual supply teachers. The meetings concentrated on the challenges of being a supply teacher, of managing it, marketing yourself, coping with the phone calls, getting the information you needed, producing check-lists for efficient and effective materials, planning and development. For the one-day supply situation in the primary school, the KIT members produced a booklet of ideas which would get supply teachers started. The booklet 'Triggers' dealt with a series of cross-curricular ideas which could be expanded if the supply work ran into more than one day.

For longer periods of supply work a series of two-day modules was developed. These started with an introductory module in which area offices and advisory teachers as well as heads shared the time and, following this, a series of two-day modules was run, focusing on single areas of the National Curriculum: mathematics, English and science. These ran and re-ran with great success. They were regularly oversubscribed and schools and participants spoke highly of the contribution they made in updating and in building confidence in participants. Economies of scale were made by using as presenters advisory teachers and others who had been involved in the National Curriculum training programme with employed teachers.

The modules represented an attempt to effect a dialogue between supply teachers and heads in planning and carrying out the training and to bring to a conscious level the requirements of headteachers of the supply teachers they employed. It was found that when heads were asked by supply teachers 'What do you want me to do?' they were vague and their answers varied enormously. Increasing the confidence of supply teachers meant that they were able to be assertive enough to go to heads and to say 'This is what I propose. Is it what you want?' The plan was to continue to offer these modules on a regular basis and to develop further across the curriculum and up through the key stages, but this process had to be curtailed because of the total removal of government funding for the project.

The Effects of LMS: The Supply Teacher Becomes a Freelance

By 1991 some LEAs had changed the picture of their supply teacher support in quite a radical way and many by that time offered some kind of support to their supply teachers. All LEAs in England were contacted by West Sussex Teacher Recruitment in the summer of 1991 and several showed a high degree of support in terms of training, access to INSET and the encouragement of self-help groups.

Berkshire devised and published a 'Code of Practice for the Employment of Supply Teachers'; East Sussex carried out some research into supply teacher issues; Croydon published and made available a 'Guide for Primary Supply Teachers' in Croydon. Surveys on the effects of the National Curriculum on supply teaching formed a focal point and Devon published booklets for headteachers and a slightly different version for supply teachers, both entitled 'Better Cover'. Here was an acknowledgment of the need for both parties to understand the perspective of the other and to work more closely together.

The Isle of Wight concentrated on 'Information for Supply Teachers' and Norfolk entitled their booklet 'A Secondary Supply Teachers' Survival Kit'. Sandwell attempted to raise awareness through their 'Information on Supply Teachers' and Wolverhampton's 'Guidance for Supply Teachers and Education Establishments' provided guidelines and codes of practice.

At the same time, the recession began to bite deeply and teacher vacancies fell. In periods of economic difficulty recruitment to initial teacher training is always buoyant and the colleges began to more than fill their initial teacher training courses. Licensed teacher routes and an increase in shortened courses contributed to improving the supply of teachers as did the government advertising campaign and the hard work that LEAs and the Teaching as a Career Unit (TASC) had been carrying out over the previous five years. Inevitably, supply work began to be harder to get, and this was further emphasized by the advent of LMS. Each supply teacher now carries a price tag: the more experienced teachers are, therefore, more expensive.

When schools became responsible for paying supply teachers out of their own budgets the amount of supply teaching available decreased. They have become more reluctant to call supply teachers and have adopted a variety of strategies to cope with their new responsibilities. Some schools cut supply teachers out of the agenda altogether and offered staff extra payments for an agreement to do extra cover. Suddenly supply teachers found themselves called in, not for a day or half a day, but for odd hours. Some supply teachers arrived at school having been called in the night before, only to be told that they were no longer needed: other arrangements had been made. Classes were split in some schools in an attempt to save money and to cut down on the amount of supply cover needed. Some schools have used their regular (and top-of-the-pay-scale) supply teachers where the cover is related to nationally funded in-service training and employ lower paid supply teachers for occasions on which they have to pay the bill.

The advantages and disadvantages of these strategies recounted by supply teachers are not the purpose of this chapter: suffice it to say that they have cut quite drastically the amount of supply teaching which is available and this has serious implications both for supply teachers and for schools. The impacts on the supply teacher have been felt immediately: the impact on the schools and pupils has yet to work its way though the system.

For the potential returner using supply teaching as a way of re-entering the classroom a dearth of supply work has meant that gaining classroom experience is now much more difficult than it was. Of course there is still the option of carrying out voluntary work but, in an atmosphere of large fields and keen competition for posts, headteachers look for substantial and regular paid classroom contact as an indication of a returner's ability to cope.

For the supply teacher who wants to use supply teaching as a source of regular income the financial results have been drastic. One such teacher told me that she had earned £600 in November 1991 and nothing at all in the same month in 1992. People working freelance expect fluctuations in their earnings but, given that the teaching year involves only forty weeks, a supply teacher has less leeway than other freelances since there are already twelve unproductive weeks in the year in terms of income. Some well-established supply teachers who have an ongoing relationship with one or two local schools have noticed little change but they are in the minority and many supply teachers or potential supply teachers may have to look elsewhere for their income.

As long as there is recession, there is some form of protection for the schools. Supply teachers may like to earn a living elsewhere but choice is limited in times of economic difficulty. When opportunities become available, however, the supply teacher may find it more convenient to have a reliable source from a part-time post outside teaching. This is the position we were in in 1986 when the KIT scheme was set up. The task then was to identify potential returners and to woo them back from other forms of employment as well as encouraging them back after a career break into the profession they had left.

The pool of teachers who are not teaching is shrinking and is expected to be one quarter of its 1990 size by the end of the decade, which means that there will be fewer supply teachers to call on (Mellor, 1992). Supply teachers have found themselves faced with the kinds of dilemmas which are common in the world of the freelance. This indicates a change in their status, for they were moving from a semi-protected environment where the help and support of the LEA could be called on to a fully independent status. This phenomenon reflects developments elsewhere: the whole field of education is about to use freelances as never before. Full-time staff in LEAs are being slimmed down; independent inspectors form some inspection teams and consultants are used for in-service training. The supply teacher will become one more freelance among a growing number of others and will have to cope with all the difficulties as well as the opportunities that such a status brings.

Already agencies exist whose lists compete with those from the LEA and concern has been expressed in the press about the adequacy of police and other checks where supply teachers come through agencies. This reflects a period of adjustment: although many other areas of employment have worked with freelances for many years, teaching has not been one of them. The LEA provided a system for identifying, making available and dealing with payments of supply teachers, and in recent years LEAs had developed training, guidance and support for supply teachers. However, much of the money was derived from the Grants for Education, Support and Training (GEST) Section 9 (Teacher Recruitment) which was removed from 1993 and most of the support disappeared with it.

LEA systems were able to be flexible enough to deal with swings in supply and demand: where shortage became acute, emergency lists of teachers who had not completed any period of employment as a teacher (previously described as those who had not completed a probationary year) and teachers who were past retirement age (and were not normally included on supply teacher lists) could be called on.

Conclusion

The future of the supply teacher is closely bound up with the future of LEAs and of the whole education service. If there is a notion of an integrated service supply teachers are an integral part of it. In West Sussex they had already begun to gain some of the benefits and responsibilities other professionals in the field have: support networks, access to INSET, specific in-service training to meet their needs. They were moving towards others: job descriptions, more accountability and a clearer understanding of their responsibilities.

In the late 1980s and early 1990s there were LEAs who had made strides in acknowledging the classroom skills needed by supply teachers and in making the teaching force aware of their responsibilities in working with supply teachers. Further development in terms of career development plans for supply teachers would include career structure, appraisal, advice and counselling. These seem unlikely, given current constraints. The mix of confidence and efficiency needed to raise the self-image of supply teachers was generated through returner and refresher activity organized by LEAs. Clarity of purpose, codes of professional practice and appropriate levels of support and training are essential elements and were becoming more commonplace. LEAs have played an important role in working towards an upward spiral of professionalization of the supply teacher role but there is a great danger that they cannot continue to play this role. Unless other mechanisms develop, with appropriate resourcing, the future must be uncertain.

References

ANONYMOUS (1989) *Teacher Shortages — A View from the Chalk Face*, Herts, the Jason Press for AMMA, NAHT, NASUWT, NUT, PAT and SHA.
BERKSHIRE DEPARTMENT OF EDUCATION (no date) 'A Code of Practice for the Employment of Supply Teachers', Berkshire LEA.
BERKSHIRE DEPARTMENT OF EDUCATION (no date) 'Supporting the Supply Teacher in Your School', Berkshire LEA.
BUZZING, P. (1989) *Keeping in Touch With Teaching: How to use the career break to prepare for your return*, HMSO.
BUZZING, P. (1989) Information Pack for Primary Supply Teachers in the Rother Valley, WSCC.

CHESSUM, L. (1989) 'The Part Time Nobody', WYCROW Working Paper 1, p. 6.
CROYDON, LONDON BOROUGH OF (no date) 'A Guide for Primary Supply Teachers'.
DEVON EDUCATION DEPARTMENT (no date) 'Better Cover', Devon County Council.
EAST SUSSEX EDUCATION DEPARTMENT (1990) 'Supporting Supply Teachers in East Sussex', East Sussex County Council.
ISLE OF WIGHT LEA (1990) 'Information for Supply Teachers'.
MELLOR, S. (1992) 'Teacher Supply in the 1990s', Unpublished text of a session at the Returners' Conference, Bromley LEA, 15 July.
NORFOLK LEA (no date) 'A Secondary Supply Teacher's Kit'.
SANDWELL LEA (no date) 'Information for Supply Teachers'.
WOLVERHAMPTON LEA (no date) 'Guidance for Supply Teachers and Educational Establishments'.

Chapter 9

The Language of Supply: A Shifting Interface for LEAs, Schools and Supply Teachers

Marlene Morrison

This chapter explores supply teaching in the context of research which took place during a period of shifting relations between local education authorities, schools, and supply teachers. It investigates assumptions which have hitherto controlled the ways in which substitution issues have been transmitted and interpreted. The author considers the extent to which language confirms approaches to absence and supply cover which marginalize supply teachers as problematic objects to be manipulated for specific ends. Whether the language of supply will change as teacher substitution is increasingly dealt with at school levels is among the issues addressed. Conclusions focus on the positive implications of re-assessing the contributions of substitute teachers viewed alongside continuing challenges for permanent colleagues and employers.

I arrived at the school the next day and was walking along the corridor to meet a new class . . . just in time to see a teacher in front of the class, tearing up the work I'd done with them the previous day. (An ex-supply teacher)

Much has been written about the professional standing of teaching over the past fifteen years. Far less attention has been given to the contributions of those who make intermittent contributions to teaching. In this chapter specific attention is drawn to the ways in which understandings about substitute teaching are defined, interpreted, transmitted, and sustained. Clarifying some of the assumptions which underpin the language of supply involves an analysis which is intentionally provocative, and includes a re-focusing on existing materials, in particular those reflected in the literature, and in responses to requests for information from local education authorities during 1991.[1]

Since it might be anticipated that supply teaching issues would be continually re-assessed in climates of compounded educational change, the initial analysis also explores the extent to which the LEA responses acknowledged or precipitated shifting locations of power and influence at school and local levels. Currently, increasing emphasis on locally managed budgets places substitute teaching among a wider range of options for school managers concerned about financial flexibility. Whether by intention or default, supply teaching issues are likely to demand a higher profile. Where organizational decision-making predominates, the question arises as to whether the language of supply confirms an instrumental view of supply teachers as 'outsiders' to be manipulated for particular ends. (Casey, 1991, notes a similar tendency when she reflects on the 'silencing' (p. 188) of professionals who leave teaching.) Alternative perspectives encourage a re-assessment of the potential and actual contribution of those who make intermittent entries to classrooms. Such assessments begin with a temporal focus.

Managing School Time

Within complex work organizations, those who manage seek to co-ordinate the activities and movement of people within them. In schools, as in other people-intensive organizations, timetables are underpinned by value and communications systems which support common expectations that, for example, teacher W will be with pupils X at time Y and for purpose Z. Teacher absence, of varying length and purpose, disturbs the temporal equilibrium which is thought to lie at the heart of 'efficient' organizations. Teacher substitution becomes part of the immediate solution to the problematic absence of a timetabled teacher.

Substitute teachers are used for a number of reasons. Depending on the situation, the practice of substituting one teacher for another is perceived differently. Secondary school pupils may 'change' teachers six or seven times a day; teacher departures for promotion, redeployment, or retirement, are accepted, even welcomed features of school life. Temporary substitution, however, tends to be viewed with a mixture of caution, regret, and sometimes alarm. Not surprisingly, negative views are more likely when the absence of the regular teacher is unanticipated, intermittent, or long-term; here, disruption to children's timetables is seen as educationally (and administratively) problematic. Education's version of the emergency trouble-shooter, highly valued in some work areas, enters school as 'the supply teacher', whose skills are at once ubiquitous and scarce, professional but 'different', and linked to perceptions about commitment, professionalism, and expectations at local and institutional levels.

A Problem for Whom?

The research aimed to answer a set of questions which treated the provision and experience of supply teaching as problematic. 'Problematic' was used in this context to establish an understanding of policy, processes, and people at a number of educational levels. (Thus initial requests for information about supply-teaching issues were posed in general terms.) Such reticence tends to be absent from recent surveys on teacher supply (for example, AMMA *et al.*, 1991, 1990). A major issue relates to the paucity of accurate statistics on supply teachers (Galloway, 1993). Equally complex are the constituent features of 'the problem' and assumptions about casual employees upon which discussions are based. In surveys, for example, supply cover issues are embedded within overall concerns about teacher supply, including vacant posts and regional and subject variations.

Research for the DES (Brown and Earley, 1990) focused on supply cover issues as essentially problematic in relation to teacher release for in-service training. Research methods were predicated on 'a situation where cover arrangements were becoming increasingly *problematic*' (op. cit., p. 4) and where research aimed 'to explore *potential problems and future issues for schools and LEAs*' (p. 4 [my emphasis]). The conclusions re-emphasized that 'there was no magic solution to the problem of cover' (op. cit., p. 39) and recommended that 'serious thought must be given to the ways in which demand for supply teachers is kept to a minimum, or which *at least ensures that their use creates as little disruption as possible*' (ibid; 1990, p. 39 [my emphasis]).

Absence, Disturbance and Substitution

In such contexts, what is meant by disruption? What the author prefers to describe as disturbance is an endemic feature of complex people-intensive organizations like schools. Using a Weberian perspective, Hassard (1988) notes that the more complex the organization becomes 'the greater the functional specialisation, and the need to synchronise and co-ordinate activities' (p. 94). Secondary schools have traditionally favoured subject specialization; more recently, primary schools have also been enjoined to develop subject-specific skills (Alexander, Rose and Woodhead 1992). This suggests that the need for teacher-specialist substitutes to replace absent colleagues is likely to remain an ongoing feature of school organizations. Viewed in this light, solutions to organizational disturbance may be not only to minimize the frequency of temporary 'aberrations' but also to promote strategies for encouraging effective learning, achievable via interchangeable professional skills among regular and intermittent teachers, and the management of teacher substitution on a continuing basis. This brings into sharper focus the specific skills required of 'temporary' professionals in organizations which are a complex mix of central control, functional specialization, and classroom autonomy. Unlike permanent colleagues, they are expected to perform a number of functions, frequently in the absence of specific knowledge about curriculum, organizational, and temporal order.

We may also need to ask: disturbance to what and for whom? Is this to pupils' learning, the routines of the school, and/or to the performance of the regular teacher? This means unpacking underlying assumptions, which include views about the negative impact of teacher substitution. Some comments have been direct and dramatic: 'We are sacrificing today's children for tomorrows' (quoted in Earley and Baker, 1989, p. 426).

A corollary might be that consistent and regular inputs sustained by one specific teacher are among the necessary criteria for effective teaching and learning. This, perhaps, sits a little uncomfortably alongside trends towards team teaching and cross-curriculum initiatives where, again, the accent is on the successful management of activities and people. Expectations are not always reflected in research evidence. Sanday (1990) draws on previous work, for example, Rutter *et al.* (1979) and Mortimore *et al.* (1988), to identify characteristics of effective schools. Whilst recognizing complex issues in analysing combined data sets, Sanday comments that:

> no correlations were found in secondary schools with stability of teacher groups, or of association of teachers with teaching groups, which is contrary to many teachers' expectations, since many primary and secondary schools make considerable efforts to maintain this degree of stability. [Rutter *et al.*, 1979, p. 133] (Sanday, 1990, p. 24)

Instead, conclusions point to the importance of purposeful leadership and the quality of teacher–pupil classroom interaction as crucial

The Language of Supply

factors. Issues of quality and disturbance linked to teacher substitution might also be related to levels of expectation by pupils, managers, and teachers, whether regular or intermittent.

Expectations

There is documented evidence to reinforce the negative implications which result from 'the cumulative effect of . . . [persistent] . . . staffing turnover on the total pattern of learning in some instances' (H.M. Inspectorate, 1989, p. 5). An HMI Report noted that:

> When there had been a succession of teachers, the planning of work had frequently been neglected and records were incomplete. In some primary schools classes with inexperienced or supply teachers, where there had been a succession of changes, the children's work and behaviour was poor . . . Rooms were . . . uninteresting, untidy and unkempt and children's work insufficiently displayed. (HM Inspectorate, 1989, p. 5)

In such cases the problem was one of succession and inconsistency, compounded by inexperience or supply cover. In contrast, among the few published accounts of supply teaching experiences, are indications that permanent teachers may themselves set boundaries and limitations as to what supply teachers might achieve. The previous extract commented on 'poor displays'; the following description in which a researcher as supply teacher describes the process of conforming to school expectations of performance, provides an alternative perspective. He writes:

> I began in earnest to replace the previous occupants' display work on the classroom wall with work done by the present class . . . When we eventually ran out of space we decided to renew the corridor display with one of our own . . . I was eventually taken aside by the acting deputy head, who informed me that he considered I'd done by far enough display work for now and that I'd 'better leave some for Mr Stewart to do when he returned' . . . I was beginning to set an unwelcome precedent, for traditionally work at 'our end of the corridor' (i.e., the upper juniors) did not involve an emphasis on display work. (Loveys, 1988, pp. 187–8)

With interest in supply cover tending to focus on the negative effects of substitution, research into the effects of colleagues' expectations on supply teacher behaviour remain sparse, yet valuable (op. cit., 1988; Nias, 1989, Morrison, in this volume). If the 'problem' of supply cover is also linked to the attitudes, behaviour, and responses of those for whom they are substitutes, then it will no longer suffice to focus solely on the negative impact of supply teaching. We must also consider the school-based organization of teaching and learning. In which case, substitute teaching is as open to research investigation as, for example, attention given to whether the removal of regular teachers for in-service training does or does not generate more effective post-INSET teaching and learning. Moreover, in educational climates where teacher appraisal continues to be debated as a complex and demanding activity, respondents in questionnaire surveys on teacher supply have been less cautious in pronouncing judgments on the 'quality' of supply teachers (AMMA *et al.*, 1990). This remains intriguing in a work situation persistently acknowledged as isolating, isolated, and not easily subject to appraisal.

What's in a Name?

A language of 'cover' which emphasizes problematic features begs at least three questions. First, is it a persistent feature of supply teaching that it attracts and/or remains available only to a 'quality' of teacher considered less than that claimed by those in permanent employment? How is 'quality' or 'lack of quality' ascertained and/or tackled? Previous research (Earley, 1986; Brown and Earley, 1990) as well as this study highlights the paucity of training for supply teachers. Second, does the practice of supply teaching demand levels of competence, confidence and flexibility more complex than those needed by permanent teachers? Among earlier commentaries is the acceptance of supply teaching as difficult and onerous. A head in one study commented: 'they need to be so good that training would not really help'! (Earley, 1986, p. 20) Paradoxically, such views coexist with alternative perspectives that supply teachers are relatively well paid for what amounts to a child-minding/holding operation (see Morrison in this volume). Finally, do comments about supply teachers reflect both gendered expectations and deficit models of casual employees, which crystallize over terms like commitment, ambition and confidence?

To date, discussion has generated contrasting images for considering such questions. The imagery rests on understandings evoked by the umbrella term 'cover' rather than the structural conditions in which 'it' and 'they' operate(s). In a now classic article linking work and the self, Hughes (1951) included the significance of occupational title for self-image, described as both 'a price tag and a calling card' (Hughes, 1951, in Esland *et al.*, 1975, p. 209). He noted, for example, that 'school teachers sometimes turn school teaching into educational work' (op. cit., p. 209). Subsequently, teachers have become managers, curriculum coordinators, incentive post-holders, pastoral heads, 'facilitators' and 'enablers'. Hughes argued that the extent to which workers endeavour to choose titles which show them in their most advantageous light 'implies an audience' and an attempt to address 'claims to be someone of worth'. Their ability to ensure that certain titles are given preference over others might also reflect their collective power *vis-à-vis* that audience. In contrast, educationalists have retained a language of supply which reflects supply teachers' individual lack of power to redefine what they do either in relation to colleagues or to clients. Flexible incentive-holders, multi-skill curriculum coordinators, cross-phase specialists, educational trouble-shooters, could be alternative titles for those persistently described as casual cover, time-sheet supply, the supply pool, or teacher substitutes. Informal teacher and pupil codes such as 'minders' or 'baby-sitters' have even more negative implications.

Pay and Conditions

The language of supply also disguises a heterogeneity in pay scales and conditions of service among those described as 'cover'. Supply teachers are employed on a day-to-day or part-day basis usually at short notice. Until recently, and in some authorities, they have also included a permanent supply pool or team, seconded or recruited specifically to facilitate coordinated planning, particularly with regard to major training initiatives of the late 1980s. Supply teachers are also drawn from those who work part-time, in some cases, working across LEA boundaries with different rates of pay and conditions of service. 'Cover' also masks a wide range of teaching experiences, from teachers working in one or a small group of schools for up to one term to those working in different schools on a daily basis. A few authorities, and some schools, have employed supply teachers as 'floating' teachers. At the start of this research, LEA supply teams probably represented the most continuously employed group among supply teachers. Evidence at local levels suggested that this was more likely in the primary than secondary sectors. In the former, supply teams had tended to be purposefully recruited; in the latter, redeployment was a more common factor. At the time of writing, financial and political exigencies cast doubts on the survival of such teams (see below). Whether or not their existence actually increased differentials among supply teachers, with 'casual supply' constituting a kind of 'under-class' in an already marginalized group, remains debatable. Paradoxically, during times of economic restraint, demands for such an 'underclass' might increase if they are seen to be cheaper than the organizational costs of retaining regular supply teams.

Hughes (1951) considered that a methodological problem in the study of work behaviour was that those who had most knowledge about an occupation were people who worked in it (Hughes, 1951, in Esland et al., 1975, p. 210). He described the use of specific words and concepts as 'blinders'. In relation to supply teaching, we might, therefore, continue to examine more carefully the 'problem' of teacher substitution and quality, ascribed to a sector of the teaching work-force in a language largely monopolized by permanent and full-time educational professionals.

Quality

At times, expectations of substitute teachers, linked to adaptability, flexibility, specialist knowledge, and control, are so high as to be inachieveable. 'Cover' has been discussed in terms of quantity, quality, and availability, and combinations of all three. Brown and Earley (1990) adopt a 'combination' stance:

> The availability of supply teachers, especially those of high quality, continues to be a problem that is unlikely to be resolved in the near future. (Brown and Earley, 1990, p. 39)

Other findings have been equally forthright:

> By far the most common worry expressed by headteachers responding with detailed comments in the survey concerned the availability and quality of supply cover. (Anonymous, 1989, p. 2)

Concerns about 'quality' will, of course, depend on the way it is viewed. In the language of supply there persists a tendency to link issues of quality to the characteristics of supply teachers themselves rather than the structural conditions in which they operate (Morrison in this volume).

Support groups, either self or LEA-generated, have been one response to such issues, either linked directly to supply teacher needs or related to wider concerns about re-activating teachers in career break situations (Mullett, 1989; Buzzing, 1989; and in this volume). Buzzing (1989) presents a picture of 'career break' women some of whom were re-entering teaching via the supply route, and who had experienced career breaks as 'a time of breaking down in confidence and in communication with the profession' (p. 1). Here, the experience of child-rearing is discussed by participants in terms of being under-valued but also impinging on individual feelings of self-worth. Buzzing's work suggests a group of returners initially vulnerable and then at pivotal phases in deciding whether supply experiences would lead to a continued career in teaching. Elsewhere, Green (in this volume) celebrates the contribution of experience in career breaks, and Evett provides a relatively optimistic picture of career-orientated primary headteachers, where:

> the availability of part-time and of supply work allow women to maintain contact with their teaching work while they are at home working as housewives/mothers. (Evetts, 1989, p. 195)

Albeit for a minority of women destined for primary headship, continuous service was not seen as a necessary pre-requisite for promotion into upper sectors of the internal labour market. She reports that 'for women in my study the break in service increased their self-confidence' (op. cit., 1989, p. 195) whilst supply teaching provided continuity.

In contrast, where 'quality' of cover is located in wider structural conditions, then both individual experience and prospects for improvement will be understood in relation to systemic aspects of school organization and career profiles. Until recently, these were occasionally reflected in strategies among some LEAs to recruit and/or contribute towards the professional development of supply staff, frequently linked to returners' schemes. Decisions to delete this area of funding from the GEST (Grants for Educational Support and Training) programme seem likely to reverse a trend whose take-up was, in any case, always patchy. Meanwhile, at school levels, whilst the negative implications of unwelcoming induction for supply staff, and positive suggestions for improved management strategies, have been

Marlene Morrison

increasingly documented (Morrison, 1993; Hufferdine, 1992), uniform prospects for improvements in pay and conditions seem unlikely.

Gender and Professionalism

Previous research has confirmed that a woman's career break produces a deterioration in career prospects relative to those in continuous employment (Martin and Roberts, 1984). In a profession with significant numbers of women, it might have been anticipated that LEAs, schools, and teachers would respond more enthusiastically to the needs and contributions of supply teachers. Two reasons suggested for a relative lack in progress are first, that managerial levels are dominated by men, and second, a view that supply teaching continues to function as:

> a second probationary period whereby teachers could sample schools and vice versa without the interference of any formal contractual obligations on either side. Just as schools could terminate a supply teacher's placement without reason, so the supply teacher could leave a school at very short notice and similarly without reason, although . . . this involved . . . more potential risk on the part of the teacher rather than the school. (Loveys, 1988, p. 180)

Moreover, Chessum (1989) notes that features of 'the gendering process', in which mainly female teachers weave casual or part-time employment with other aspects of their lives, are masked by 'a language of professionalism' (p. 87). This:

> serves to include those women who have been able to organise their lives in a full-time way similar to men, but separates them from their part-time sisters. The perspectives of full-time women teachers are often governed by this professionalism even though they may be part-timers in the future or have been part-timers in the past. (Chessum, 1989, p. 87)

Viewed in this way female full-timers have survived the 'caring' tunnel and emerged as 'copers' with full-time 'commitment'. Chessum's study remains useful in highlighting part-time or supply-time 'commitment' as a concentrated application of teaching effort which remains distinct from domestic or child-rearing pressures (ibid., p. 76).

During 1991 local education authorities were contacted by the author for outlines of policies on supply teaching. Their responses provided an important backdrop for considering these and other perceptions about supply teaching issues.

Local Voices

Thirty-three responses and subsequent meetings with LEA representatives offered regional and local perspectives on supply cover. At the start of the project these reflected both a range of organizational approaches and pending changes as financial budgets were devolved to schools. In some respects, responses reflected the *ad hoc* arrangements and diversity noted previously (Earley, 1986), and differences in philosophies and/or staffing levels. Requests for information were addressed to directors of education or chief education officers. Eleven responses were from that level; of the remainder it was interesting to note that many respondents had the words 'recruitment', 'retention' and/or 'personnel' included in their titles, also reflecting a shifting, if transient emphasis on teacher supply at that time. Titles ranged from those as specific as 'coordinator of teaching recruitment initiatives' to 'recruitment manager'. Two respondents identified themselves as members of school middle management seconded by their authorities to 'sort out' supply and its organizational arrangements. Several authorities had prepared or were preparing introductory packs for supply teachers and guidelines for schools. More significantly, the responses indicated shifting definitions of responsibilities and practice as aspects of changing staffing, financial, and political circumstances. Some authorities had a surplus of permanent teachers in situations of falling school rolls; others were using supply to cover for existing deficiencies. Of course, no claims are made that the initial responses encapsulated all that was happening or not happening in those authorities. Negotiated entry into two authorities for the detailed case studies allowed a closer examination. At the end of the project, the curtailed role of LEAs meant that most aspects of supply provision would be devolved to schools. What follows, then, is also the language of the interim, with its sense of uncertainty about future priorities.

Seven authorities discussed supply as a problem or as a problematic issue: this was expressed in a number of ways and with varying emphasis on a continuum from central direction to relative autonomy at school levels. Authorities which stressed positive action affirmed the need for continuing efforts to 'increase availability' and 'improve quality'. Cost was emphasized specifically by those authorities which ran both central registers and/or had permanent supply teams. Two authorities were keen to emphasize that 'we do not have a problem'. Both related the absence of a 'problem' to availability rather than quality. One respondent acknowledged a continuing need to consider '[supply teachers'] National Curriculum training . . .' and that it 'planned to give training in SATs . . . to supply teachers'.

For two authorities, specifically in relation to secondary supply, the creation of supply teams had solved a problem, namely that of preventing compulsory redundancies, whilst facilitating a more effective organization of teacher release for in-service training. Writing in 1991, one respondent commented on 'protecting teachers from compulsory redundancy' for an operational span of 'at least the next 2–3 years'. Similarly, an interview with an authority representative indicated that solving one problem had delayed the onset of another. In this case, secondary supply teachers were displaced teachers; with a cut in educational budget for 1991–2, the team was being disbanded. It was increasingly difficult to persuade senior school management to re-employ displaced teachers who might have been released with least reluctance in the first place. Retirement and compulsory redundancies were the remaining options. It appeared that in such cases supply teaching was a staging post into permanent teaching after a career break, and out of teaching prior to redundancy or retirement.

Among the responses were several accounts of strenuous efforts to improve the efficiency, quality and quantity of supply cover, even if 'positive action does not eliminate all of the problems'. One document observed that:

> The basic philosophy is to regard [supply] team members as adaptable and prepared to tackle any situation positively. Nevertheless, there has, on occasions, been a 'mismatch' of expectations and the incoming teacher has been regarded as merely a 'baby sitter'. Work left on occasions was less than adequate; on the other hand . . . [schools] . . . have indicated that team members have not always grasped the teaching opportunities open to them. (LEA document provided to the CEDAR Research Team, 1991)

Teacher association responses took a Janus-like stance to supply, adopting both the perspective of supply teachers on pay and conditions and school-focused positions on availability and quality. Few other respondents perceived issues from the perspective of substitute teachers.

There were exceptions, including examples of authority-wide interest, sometimes sparked by a core of supply teachers. Large authorities emphasized organizational and administrative issues in keeping supply lists up-to-date, accurate, and regularly circulated; one respondent reflected on a variety of approaches used in different areas within the same authority.

Only one authority used the term 'disruption' in the context of negative implications for 'school routine', but stopped short of making those implications specific. Three authorities were also prepared to discuss or comment on geographical disparities, particularly in relation to availability:

> A large number of supply teachers are in theory available for work in the area [X], but once the name of the school is given their diaries appear to become more problematic. (An LEA education division statement, 1990)

Among positive responses was a pilot scheme to attract supply teachers into a specific area within one authority. Supply teachers were recruited to serve a cluster of primary schools. Here, supply teachers qualified for a bonus payment of £50 after teaching the equivalent of ten days in schools within their cluster. In addition, each supply teacher who attended a training day during the pilot period was paid a salary allowance of £20.

Walking — Talking — Breathing

In the choice of vocabularies used by some respondents there is something of an 'as-long-as-they-can-walk-talk-and-breathe' flavour about recruitment which reflects some of the wider images of supply teachers. This was particularly evident in relation to 'casual' workers on central registers, described intriguingly by several authorities as *ad hoc* teachers. The criminal record check seemed the constant and minimum requirement. Qualified teacher status, post-probationary and pre-retirement conditions were the more flexible criteria, and varied widely. For example, an LEA respondent commented that:

> the Authority has no specific policy for the recruitment of supply teachers. Requests are received from a variety of teachers seeking regular, often part-time work.

In an admittedly brief response, there was little indication of the terms upon which 'the request' was accepted, and as long as schools were 'aware', 'the Authority also employs newly trained teachers who have not passed the probationary period'. Another representative noted that 'we recruit anyone who meets the basic requirements of satisfactory references, medical clearance and criminal disclosure'. Apparently the only other group to be excluded were those 'who might have retired on the grounds of ill-health'.

More vigorous and career-orientated policies had been pursued in those authorities which had encouraged supply teams and/or returners' schemes. This was especially evident with regard to interview procedures, and served to highlight further the hierarchical gradations within an employment sector described generally as supply cover. Two authorities interviewed everyone on their lists; five interviewed applicants for either or both primary and secondary supply teams. Those on career break schemes might or might not be interviewed. And of course, the largest group of 'unknowns' remained those recruited individually by schools.

During 1991, with increasing attention given to recruitment and retention, and supported by GEST funding (DES, 1990, pp. 46–8), more LEAs were engaged in returners' schemes; these included programmes of professional development for re-entrants or mature entrants, among whom were those likely to take the 'supply' route. One authority with an affluent catchment and high local housing costs had identified a pool of inactive teachers, already located in the LEA as a result of domestic partnerships with those whose earnings allowed them to reside there. Encouraging women returners in career breaks was seen partly as a pragmatic response to recruitment in an area which might otherwise experience difficulties in gaining new entrants on lower salary scales. Doing supply work was one route back to permanent teaching; strategies to discourage negative supply teaching experiences were, therefore, critically focused. In two authorities, professional development and supply teaching were being encouraged by the provision of child-care allowances. Overall, however, organized training for supply teachers was rare, although a few authorities were clearly pursuing this more vigorously than others.

Future Roles

The most striking feature to emerge from responses was a snapshot of authorities at various stages in deciding their future roles in teacher supply. This was enmeshed within ongoing pressures on educational budgets and increased financial delegation to schools. It crystallized over the issue of whether 'permanent' supply teams would continue, in situations where the financial burden of maintaining full-time teams was proving too great for most authorities, as the following comment from an LEA spokesperson suggests:

> The position since 1988 has changed significantly. With the onset of local financial management, coupled with major changes in INSET funded by the DES, the education department has had to review the position of teams which, throughout their existence, were meant to be self-financing. The secondary team has been scaled down, and during the past-year replacements to the primary team have been appointed on a fixed-term-contract basis only. It is anticipated by March 1992 INSET supply cover will once more be engaged on an *ad hoc* basis only, and this innovation which has enabled schools to participate in an intensive programme of day-time provision will have run its course.

Similar events were occurring in other authorities but over shorter time-scales. One recruitment manager was 'counselling' the supply team back into schools; the primary team in another authority was being similarly redeployed, whilst the secondary team was taking retirement and redundancy routes. In one authority, recruitment to supply teams 'has been temporarily disbanded pending further developments in local management of schools and delegation of budgets'. Two representatives informed the researcher that from 1991 schools would arrange their own supply cover, noting 'indications ... that this will increase the tendency to use models of in-service provision which lessen the need for teacher release during school time'.

A few authorities still anticipated a role in strategic planning as one among several ways of retaining important ties between themselves and schools in the face of diminishing links elsewhere. In a specific example, an LEA recorded its attempts to stabilize that relationship. It operated a relief-cover team which consisted of seventy-three Full-Time Equivalent teachers, of whom 52.3 were in the primary sector. Following a policy review the latter was reduced to forty-two in April 1991. The relatively smaller size of the secondary team reflected the option that secondary schools had taken in enhancing their staffing to provide cover. In 1991, schools without delegated powers were expected to participate in the scheme. Schools paid a non-recouperable base charge for the year to take into account cost factors

Marlene Morrison

like: team member absence, under use, car mileage, advertising, IN-SET recruitment, and administration. (Team members had administrative bases in schools.) The authority stressed that the continuity of a well-trained supply team would depend on the numbers who 'opted in'. In March 1991 primary schools with delegated budgets were asked to indicate whether they wished to opt in for the year 1991–2. Of those with the option to do so, more than two-thirds had opted in by May 1991. The team was retained but with reduced levels of staffing. Subsequently, the secondary-school team would be disbanded during 1992.

At the end of the project it was clear that this kind of employment-agency role for LEAs was to be severely curtailed. By June 1991, LEA perspectives on teacher supply and cover issues showed wide disparities in organization and planning. These continued to fluctuate as financial and political constraints moved them in a number of directions, despite advice to 'review what [could] be done in each case [of cover, supply teachers, and the recruitment of returners], and adopt the appropriate best practice' (Interim Advisory Committee on School Teachers' Pay and Conditions, 1991, p. 24). Currently, their role consists primarily of vetting supply teachers' records, allocating funds to cover regular teachers' training, and paying supply (and short-term contract) teachers. Schools are now most likely to make the offer of employment on an occasional basis and deploy staff as appropriate. This is leading to an increasingly heterogeneous market, and disparate conditions of employment for those engaged at education's periphery. During 1991–2, there was evidence that some LEAs were grouping together to coordinate marketing and publicity strategies for encouraging a wider recruitment and retention of staff. With the end of GEST funding, prospects for collaborative action look far less promising. In times of reorganization at the meso level and increased complexity of educational tasks at the micro level, LEA activity during the interim suggests an even greater need to find a new discourse for supply themes.

Alternative Perspectives

Lukes (1974) reminds us that 'power operates within a particular moral and political perspective . . .' and 'involves endless disputes about its proper use' (p. 26). In the educational world of the 1990s such perspectives are dominated by accountability and rationalization (Stenning, 1990, p. 172). The language of supply reflects such perspectives.

Research reveals contradictions and paradoxes. Teacher substitutes have been deployed to facilitate a process whereby those for whom they substitute become more accountable. To achieve this, an amoeba-like group of casual workers has been needed to expand and contract as the twin demands for accountability and rationalization have grown. The implications of such demands have remained partially hidden as the essence of the problem is seen less in terms of teaching and learning by regular or by supply teachers, but more on the need to ensure that the amoeba remains mobile, flexible and large enough to support the organisms which feed on it. The language of supply also rests on the ability and/or inclination of the amoeba to respond to the multiplicity of demands made on it. The organization of teaching and learning; the experiences and conditions faced by casual workers; the effects of their relationships with permanent teachers; and of both groups upon pupils and vice versa; these remain secondary to hierarchical concerns about availability, quality and cost.

In earlier work, the author argued that Atkinson's model of 'a flexible work-force' (Atkinson, 1984) was a useful starting point for understanding educational employment, specifically the experiences of its casual and part-time workers in the late 1980s (Morrison, 1989). More recently, Stenning (1990) makes a similar point when he examines the prospects for school-staff employment in the 1990s. Atkinson's model rests on assertions about the need for work-force flexibility in times of economic recession, market uncertainty, and changes in product and production methods. To respond and to survive such changes, organizations, including those in education, need first, functional flexibility, achievable by employing workers who are willing and able to adapt to new forms of work; second, numerical flexibility through the organization's ability to vary the size of the work-force or the numbers of hours worked in response to changes in demand; and third, financial flexibility to allow costs to be related to the external labour market. Such flexibility is achieved by the segmentation of the organization into difference sectors, a core and a periphery, the former providing functional flexibility and the latter numerical flexibility. In 1990,

> there [is] already the fairly widespread practice of employing teachers on short-term contracts in accordance with current demand, and the strong tradition for buttressing core staff with supply teachers bears testimony to the presence of . . . [a] . . . peripheral group among the teaching force for many years past. (Stenning, 1990, p. 175)

The core group of permanent teachers remains core as long as its members accept that their functional flexibility will be subject to ongoing re-assessment and appraisal over a wide 'range of prescribed activities' (op. cit., p. 175); this might include the provision and organization of their own professional development as long as other priorities are deemed more pressing. With changing conditions of employment, and prospects for locally and individually negotiated rates of pay, permanent teachers remain a precarious 'core'. Recommendations to reduce supply cover and concentrate on alternative strategies for both cover and in-service training (for example, Brown and Earley, 1990) could increase the pressure on the 'core' for flexibility over an even wider range of teaching and non-teaching duties, especially when financial considerations reinforce a view of supply teaching as the 'last resort' option. In choosing to ignore the experienced reality of supply teaching other than in a language which emphasizes disruption and individual deficiencies, we neglect a vital group of teachers whose conditions may eventually be shared by many in the existing 'core'. Meanwhile, as Stenning (1990) has argued, 'in the annals of British labour relations a characteristic feature has been an overriding concern with symptoms and the immediate solution of perceived ills' (p. 176).

Conclusion

The language of supply has tended to promote a view of supply teaching as a temporarily expedient, if problematic response, to teacher absence from the classroom. Local financial management may lend further weight to the view that the cost of supply cover outweighs its benefits for teachers and for pupils. If this proves to be the case, future balance sheets of educational costs and benefits may also need to consider the deleterious effects, upon teachers and pupils, of core teachers being asked to cover for absent colleagues. As LEAs struggle to maintain their strategic role in planning teacher supply, it would be ironic if more imaginative strategies for the support and development of substitute teachers arose not from their existing or potential contributions at the chalk-face but in response to a growing recognition that the conditions of service for increasing numbers of regular teachers resemble those of their colleagues at the periphery. At LEA level, even the most realistic implications of recent research stand little chance of being implemented. Nevertheless, evidence led the research team (Burgess, Galloway, and Morrison) to conclude that minimum ways forward need to include regional collaboration, reliable data bases, support for supply teacher training, and the coordination of information which, for those working occasionally, remains critical. Each provides frameworks for diagnosis which move beyond existing vocabularies to consider the wider and longer term educational implications of a shifting interface of power and influence as it affects, and is reflected in, supply teaching.

Note

1 This formed part of a research project entitled Supply Teaching in English Schools: An Investigation of Policy Processes and People, funded by the Leverhulme Trust and conducted by R.G. Burgess, S. Galloway, and M. Morrison at the Centre for Educational Development, Appraisal and Research (CEDAR) at the University of Warwick, during 1991–2.

References

ALEXANDER, R., ROSE, J. and WOODHEAD, C. (1992) *Curriculum Organisation and Classroom Practice in Primary Schools: a Discussion Paper*, London, DES.

AMMA (1991) 'Newsline — Supply Teaching: 4 Teacher Articles', in *Report*, 13, 5, March.

AMMA, NAHT, NASUWT, NUT, PAT and SHA (1990) *Report of Joint Union Survey on Teacher Shortages: September 1990*, London, Jevons Brown.

ANONYMOUS (1989) *Teacher Shortages — A View From the Chalk Face*, Herts, the Jason Press for AMMA, NAHT, NASUWT, NUT, PAT and SHA.

ATKINSON, J. (1984) *Flexibility, Uncertainty and Manpower Management*, Brighton, Institute of Management Studies.

BROWN, S. and EARLEY, P. (1990) *Enabling Teachers to Undertake Inservice Education and Training*, A Report for the DES, Slough, NFER.

BUZZING, P. (1989) *Keeping in Touch with Teaching*, London, HMSO.

CASEY, K. (1991) 'Why do progressive women activists leave teaching: Theory, methodology and politics in life history research', in GOODSON, I. (Ed.) *Studying Teachers' Lives*, London, Routledge.

CHESSUM, L. (1989) *The Part-time Nobody*: Part-time women teachers in West Yorkshire, Yorkshire, WYCROW.

DES (1990) *Grants for Educational Support and Training 1991–1992*. (GEST) Draft Circular 20, July.

EARLEY, P. (1986) *Questions of Supply: an exploratory study of external cover arrangements*, Slough, NFER.

EARLEY, P. and BAKER (1989) 'Supply and Demand: Finding solutions to the problem of cover', in *Education*, 5 May, pp. 426–7.

ESLAND, G., SALAMAN, G. and SPEAKMAN, M.A. (Eds) (1975) *People and Work*, Edinburgh, Holmes McDougall for the Open University Press, Milton Keynes.

EVETTS, J. (1989) 'The Internal Labour Market for Primary Teachers' in ACKER, S. (Ed.) (1989) *Teachers, Gender and Careers*, Lewes, The Falmer Press.

GALLOWAY, S. (1993) '"Out of Sight, Out of Mind": A response to the literature on supply teaching', in *Educational Research*, 35, 2, Summer.

HASSARD, J. (1988) 'Time and Organisation', in BLYTON, A.P., HASSARD, J., HILL, S. and STARKEY, K., *Time, Work and Organisation*, London, Routledge.

HM INSPECTORATE (1989) *Teacher Supply in Seventeen Schools in Tower Hamlets and Wandsworth*, London, DES.

HUFFERDINE, J. (1992) 'Temporary Accommodations', in *Managing Schools Today*, 1, 8, June.

HUGHES, E. (1951) 'Work and the Self', in ESLAND, G., SALAMAN, G. and SPEAKMAN, M.A. (1975) *People and Work*, Holmes McDougall for the Open University Press, Milton Keynes.

INTERIM ADVISORY COMMITTEE ON SCHOOL TEACHERS' PAY AND CONDITIONS (1991) *Fourth Report of the Interim Advisory Committee on School Teachers' Pay and Conditions*, Chairman: Lord Chilver, London, HMSO, 18 January.

LOVEYS, M. (1988) 'Supplying the Demand? Contract, mobility and institutional location in the changing world of the supply teacher' in OZGA, J. (Ed.) *School Work: Approaches to the Labour Process of Teaching*, Milton Keynes, Open University Press.

LUKES, S. (1974) *Power: A: Radical View*, Basingstoke, Macmillan.

MARTIN, J. and ROBERTS, C. (1984) *Women and Employment — A Lifetime Perspective*, London, HMSO.

MORRISON, M. (1989) 'An Exploration of the Meanings of Part-time, for those who experience it in a college of further education', Unpublished M.Ed. thesis, University of Warwick.

MORRISON, M. (1993) 'Running for Cover: Substitute Teaching and the Secondary Curriculum', in *Curriculum*, 14, 2, pp. 125–39.

MORTIMORE, P., SAMMON, P., STOLL, L., LEWIS, D. and ECOB, E. (1988) *School Matters*, Wells, Open Books.

MULLETT, M. (1989) *Research into Supply Teacher Issues: Results and Report*, Buckinghamshire County Council Education Department.

NIAS, D.J. (1989) 'Supply, Temporary and Part-time Teachers: Partial Members of the School?', in NIAS, D.J. *Primary Teachers Talking*, London, Routledge.

RUTTER, M., MAUGHAN, B., MORTIMORE, P., OUSTON, J. and SMITH, A. (1979) *Fifteen Thousand Hours: Secondary Schools and their Effects of Children*, London, Open Books.

SANDAY, A. (1990) *Making Schools More Effective*, CEDAR Occasional Papers 2, University of Warwick, CEDAR.

STENNING, R. (1990) 'School Staff Employment Trends in the Maintained Sector: some agendas for research' in SARAN, R. and TRAFFORD, V. (Eds) *Research in Education Management and Policy: Retrospect and Prospect*, London, The Falmer Press.

Chapter 10

Supply Teaching as a Labour Market Phenomenon

Robert M. Lindley

In previous chapters the voices of experience are evident in a range of educational settings. In this chapter, readers have the opportunity to stand back and consider at the macro-level the implications of supply teaching, in particular the changing nature of the employment relationship and the distinction between internal and external labour market policies. Robert Lindley explores the ways in which the location of teaching within the occupational-organizational-industrial structure can shift in response to changes in the socio-economic environment, and offers a wider perspective on supply teachers at work in schools and classrooms.

One of the largest and most skilled occupational groups in any modern society is the teaching profession. In Britain, over the last decade and a half, it has been subject to a variety of reforms, some designed specifically to change the profession and some to change the structure and management of the educational system. Both direct and indirect reforms have, inevitably, been greeted with great concern by teachers, whether seeing themselves as guardians of the culture and quality of educational provision, as members of a profession whose power is under threat, or as employees who believe that their job satisfaction is likely to deteriorate (Grace and Lawn, 1991). In all three respects, the concern has been heightened by a widespread view among teachers that much of the change has been ill-considered in its design, hurriedly implemented, and embodies a degree of prejudice against the profession on the part of the successive Conservative governments covering this period.

In these circumstances, researchers as well as practitioners will tend to become preoccupied both with the central issues affecting the majority of teachers and with what appears to be the exceptional nature

Robert M. Lindley

of the situation in education. Yet some of the effects of policy initiatives, if not always their actual intentions, have been to produce greater differentiation within the education system whilst introducing into it modes of thinking and operation which differentiate it less than hitherto from the conduct of other employing activities in society (Stenning, 1990).

So, for example, whilst the majority of teachers now perceive and some actually experience less security of employment than in previous periods, this is a factor in common with a number of other highly qualified groups outside the education system. Moreover, it brings professional occupations closer to what has been the common experience of the majority of the working population.

This increase in uncertainty is partly transitional because of the introduction of so much change but is also partly a consequence of creating new structures within the education system that give more discretion to schools and colleges in conducting their personnel policies at the same time as giving them more discretion in the financial area.

At the beginning of this period of traumatic change, however, there were already many teachers working at the margin of educational organizations whose conditions of employment were much less favourable than those still now enjoyed by the majority of the profession. Thus this chapter, in common with the other contributions to the book, steps outside the mainstream of research on teachers by focusing on supply teaching but also introduces analytical perspectives which, whilst recognizing its particular nature within education, treats 'supply' as an example of a more generic labour market phenomenon concerned with labour flexibility and the organizational structures advanced to promote it.

The chapter[1] seeks to explore ways of analysing supply teaching which derive from some of the concepts developed in the labour market field. Given the focus of this book, it would be inappropriate to deal with the labour market for teachers as a whole. However, at various points, it will be apparent that behind the analysis lies a more general approach to the study of the position of education in the socio-economic system and the principal professional labour market associated with it. Furthermore, this in turn derives from the wider study of how societies evolve and how certain functions come to be located in particular parts of the occupational-organizational-industrial structure of the economy.

There are four main parts to the chapter: the first introduces a number of analytical concepts; the second examines the notion of 'supply teaching' from the labour market point of view; the third explores how the supply 'problem' has been structured by certain features of educational organizations some of which are optional rather than essential; the concluding part deals with the implications of the analysis for policy.

Labour Market Analysis: Some Distinctions

Several concepts have played an important part in the modern analysis of labour markets. Whilst frequently rooted in applied economics or economic sociology, such analysis is essentially multi-disciplinary if it is to lead to worthwhile scientific insights of relevance to policy. The principal analytical ideas relevant to the study of supply teachers are summarized below. Relevance to the context of the education system and, to some degree, supply teaching is illustrated in the accompanying tables.

Functions, Organizations and Markets

Organizations and groups of organizations can be seen to perform a range of functions. Some organizations which produce the same product or service do not always perform the same functions in order to achieve this. In particular, the choice between what to purchase from others and what to provide internally will depend on many factors. History as well as current economic situation and organizational strategies play a part in most explanations.

It has been suggested (Lindley, 1987) that there is an incipient 'functional relocation' taking place in the European economy in which certain functions appear to be shifting their location in the organizational-industrial structure. This could well increase in significance but international evidence indicates that it is much more apparent in some countries than in others. Theoretical work has, nonetheless, tended to deal with very simple notions of organizational structure and this reduces its utility in analysing periods of change characterized by shifts in organization — market relationships. The notion of 'function' must interpose between outputs and inputs in the traditional economic treatment of the organization. The theory then needs to be re-cast in terms of an organization choosing its product market strategy, which functions to perform itself, and which to purchase via the market system. In a period of major change, many of these choices are re-examined

> - the functions to be performed by the State education system are being more precisely defined in terms of inputs, outputs and processes;
> - the LEA's functions as an employment organization are being reduced in favour of its functions as a potential supplier of services to teaching establishments;
> - schools and colleges are becoming *de-facto* employing organizations as well as teaching establishments;
> - but LEAs retain certain controls over the exercise of power at establishment level;
> - it remains to be seen how much LEA control in the areas of finance, personnel and educational standards will provide them with influence capable of being deployed in the supply of services; and
> - it is likely, however, that the position of the LEAs in the new system will lend a transactions' cost advantage to their supplying services in competition with other suppliers.

Table 1: *Functional Relocation in Education*

and altered, meaning that the economy exhibits structural change at a deeper level than is normal. The phenomenon has not been restricted to the business sector; the role of the state in providing services to the public and the choice of organizational form for this purpose has been much discussed, especially in Britain.

Sometimes, new organizations emerge specializing in a particular function and supplying it to customer organizations who previously provided it internally; sometimes customer organizations decide to perform functions they previously purchased outside. The former is a case of externalization, the latter — internalization. Research and development, transportation, cleaning, software development, and training are among the many functions that have been the subject of externalization, internalization or both.

There are also organizations which may be called 'agencies' that specialize in supplying not so much the full service of a function but the people with capacities that enable them to provide a function from within the framework of a customer organization but as an employee of the agency rather than the customer.

During the last decade or so there has been much debate about the development of more flexible organizational structures, leading to the growth of different forms of employment status. Despite publicity given to a variety of experiments the evidence for substantial change is rather weak. The only marked growth in the number of organizations using such strategies has been in sub-contracting, a phenomenon associated with that of externalization noted above (Casey, 1988; Millward and Stevens, 1986; Millward *et al.*, 1992). However, there is evidence of some organizations increasing the extent to which they use non-regular employment, especially part-time contracts.

- LEAs as employers have operated rather weak forms of internal labour market, only asserting 'employer-like' authority in times of major rationalization;
- the reforms have formally decentralized personnel decision-making to the schools;
- the future of the wider, internal labour market depends on LEAs retraining and developing responsibility for the overall personnel framework;
- the role of the LEA in responding to supply problems and training needs will be the acid test of whether an extension of the external labour market for teachers replaces the weak internal market existing hitherto; and
- both these latter activities may be coordinated by non-LEA agencies with schools directly contracting with them to provide management advice and operational support.

Table 2: Re-orientation of External and Internal Labour Markets for School Teachers

Notions of External and Internal Markets

The existence of organizations which are highly structured provides for the development of quasi-market transactions which are internal to the organization. Recognition of these alongside external market transactions between different legal entities is essential to an understanding of the evolution of the modern economy.

By the same token internal labour markets exist in which mobility between jobs can rival that observed via external labour markets (about half of regional labour mobility, for example, actually takes place without a change of employer). The structuring of internal labour markets can, moreover, have a profound effect upon external labour markets by restricting entry to jobs in parts of the occupational spectrum to those promoted from within rather than recruited directly and by denying non-employees access to training in these occupational areas.

Education and Training Markets

The very close association between access to training and entry into a contractual relationship with an employer has tended to blur the distinction between the markets for training and labour (Lindley, 1991a). Yet in analysing the nature of labour shortages it is essential to recognize the potentially separate roles of the two markets and to recognize that they need not be so integrated as they are in certain parts of the economy, such as in training for craft occupations in engineering or (until recently) for nursing, both being examples of employer-driven training provision.

Furthermore, even where employer-based training provision is dominant, the distinction between funding and supplying education and training should be maintained. The physical capacity of employers to supply training may be harnessed in a regime in which the cost is borne by the state or, indeed, by the individual.

Finally, the distinction between 'general' and 'specific' training is frequently recognized. The former relates to training which improves the potential performance of the employee in a very wide range of possible organizations and the latter relates to training which improves the performance of the individual primarily in a particular organization. Employers, it is argued, will then concentrate upon funding specific training, leaving the state or individual to fund general training (where the risk of loss of investment return is greatest). More complex options can be recognized however, in that it may be economically quite rational for an employer to fund general training because the specific training being given is sufficient to lock the employee into the organization or, for social or geographical reasons, the worker is relatively immobile.

Small organizations are particularly vulnerable to loss of return on investment in training. This is because their position in the product market yields little market power by which to pass on a share of high profits to employees in the form of high wages and better conditions of employment. The risks of trained personnel leaving to join other organizations is therefore greater. In addition, the economies of scale in providing training to large numbers and opportunities for using internal cover for training are much lower than in large organizations.

Strategic behaviour by departments within organizations which have introduced cost or profit centres can reproduce in the internal labour market the same economic tensions over whether or not to fund training as those described above in the external labour market context.

Internalization versus Externalization: The Case of Training

A major policy issue in the vocational training field is the extent to which training should be an integral part of the employment relationship (internalization) or whether it should be supplied independently (externalization). In the first case, the markets for labour and training operate jointly with employment contracts involving explicit or implicit commitments on the parts of employers to provide training and the employee to undergo it. In some instances, the costs of training are borne entirely by the employer and in others, they are shared by the employee.

In the second case, the training and labour markets operate separately, though they interact. The essential point is that access to, and financial support for, training are not exclusively secured via an employment relationship. Individuals may obtain training which is fully recognized in the labour market and may have significant opportunities for financial support, both quite independently of an employer.

Government may choose to foster the development of one market structure rather than another. Equity as well as efficiency considerations may influence the balance of policy. In Britain, there has been a tendency to neglect the individual perspective in the field of adult training; governments have quite explicitly taken the view that this is a matter for employers whereas initial training across a wide range of occupations should be a joint responsibility of the new employer and the state (Lindley, 1991b).

The case against externalization is that it promotes remoteness between the needs of the job and the training made available and it relies too much on the individual's motivation and judgment of the risks. The case against internalization is that it produces low-quality training continually under threat from operational pressures of the job and that it relies too much on the employer's motivation and judgment of risk.

A compromise between the two is external 'certification' of training which remains dominated by internal labour market provision. The certification maintains quality; internalization maintains relevance to the employer, ensures financial support for the individual, and reduces the risk perceived by the individual, because little personal cost is incurred and the training is obviously recognized to be worthwhile by at least the current employer.

But this still leaves the problem of motivating the employer: training is costly, well-trained employees may leave and a substantial part of the returns on a investment may be lost. Indeed external certification will tend to increase the risk to the employer because it typically raises the average standard of training and the costs involved. Moreover, even when employers agree to raising the quality there is then a danger that they will subsequently lower the volume of training more sharply than might otherwise have been the case during cyclical downturns or other forms of financial stringency. During the 1960s and 1970s, employers were educated to appreciate the importance of sustaining expenditure on high-quality training as a long-run investment: sadly whilst the rhetoric of the good times appeared to suggest that attitudes were changing, the reality of the bad times revealed that short-run financial imperatives still held sway.

Even the experience of the last decade has been that training volume and quality will suffer without both a central subsidy and a regulatory agency with the mission to provide transparently common standards in key areas of training and with the power to operate a 'levy-grant' system of some kind in favour of companies achieving those standards (Ryan, 1991).

The 'internalization' option is then a training strategy which can only work with a substantial external support system. Otherwise it appears to degenerate into below-optimal volumes and quality of training over the long-term and above-optimal variations in the adjustment of training activity according to the current needs of the organization for qualified workers.

Similarly, the 'externalization' option requires not only the creation of an external market structure for training separated from employment but also access to the training capacities of employing organizations. The distinction between funding and provision is a critical one. Externalization of training does not require a mass programme to create a completely new physical capacity for training in the form of the buildings and equipment of new training schools and a new cadre of trainers to go with them. However, the essence of a shift towards greater externalization is the provision and take-up of a much larger proportion of training places to which access is obtained without the employer acting as gate-keeper. Existing employers with spare training capacity, or who decided to enter the training business as a secondary activity by increasing their capacity beyond that required to meet internal demands, could enter the training market.

Job Content and the Social Construction of Occupations

Analysis of labour markets is clouded by the extent to which job content varies both between apparently identical occupations in similar organizations and over time. To some degree, all jobs are re-designed by the new incumbent and many vacancies provide opportunities for employers and, indeed, collaborating employees to alter the range of tasks conducted or the balance between them. More broadly, occupations are essentially socially constructed, reflecting the outcome not simply of an organizational and technological logic but of power and interest in labour and product markets and the wider society.

The notion of function has been introduced in order to clarify the analysis of occupations and to relate it to structural change in the

> - schools, like small enterprises, will find it difficult to commit themselves to the volume and quality of staff training required — training budgets will be continually under pressure;
> - raising the quality of training will threaten the volume because teacher training is mainly 'general' — applicable to many schools;
> - in theory, some schools could enter the 'training business' as an activity which is viable in itself covering initial training and/or continuing training and staff development;
> - could a role as trainers/tutors for experienced supply teachers then evolve?;
> - however, government experimentation with different forms of initial teacher training involving more school-based training is taking place when the schools are becoming the kinds of organizations least likely to sustain such an activity alongside their main function (on which management work load is still increasing);
> - commitments to continuing education of existing staff and other teachers not currently employed are also under threat; and
> - LEAs or equivalent agencies would seem to be necessary to re-introduce through coordination the benefits from training otherwise denied to a collection of small organizations.

Table 3: Staff Training Relating to Schools

economy. Three sets of distinctions are advocated, dealing with the relationships:

- between function and occupation;
- between shifts in the way a function is organized which alter jobs sufficiently to be recorded as changes in occupational data (as conventionally classified) and those where much significant change in job content is not captured in such data; and
- between skills actually employed, entry requirements for a job, and qualifications held by the individual doing a job.

The functions should then represent underlying activities rather than the way in which they are carried out via occupations. The skills should represent the abilities and experience needed to do the jobs created in the occupational hierarchy rather than the formal educational qualifications or other vocational training conditions used as minimum entry requirements or held by the 'average person' in the occupation.

In many jobs, not just those high up the occupational hierarchy, there is considerable scope to adjust the content of work carried out in a particular occupation and in other occupations interacting with it or the capital equipment and materials it employs where the time-structure of tasks involved allows for considerable transient substitution, or where performance standards are not easily monitored. Skills/occupations are essentially socially constructed rather than being

> - an intensification in the job content of teaching posts has occurred;
> - at the same time, teachers perceive a loss of professional control and an increase in stress;
> - the functions performed by teachers have been extended, especially those of senior staff with respect to management;
> - most supply teachers experience problems with defining their role; and
> - school occupational structures are under some pressure to change partly through financial difficulty but also because new choices are now available for substitution.

Table 4: Job Content and School Occupational Structures

determined by the logic of operational necessity. Professional bodies particularly seek to maintain occupational boundaries which suit the interests of their members.

A central analytical problem relates to the treatment of autonomy and control in examining changing job quality. It is clear that in most countries there is a relative growth of intermediate and higher-level occupations. The resulting jobs appear to offer more opportunities for personal discretion over the planning, organization and execution of work tasks. However, amongst some of these groups, there have been developments leading to a greater degree of control being imposed upon them from both within the employing organization and beyond it. The debate about the extent to which clerical work has been 'proletarianized' has extended to encompass more qualified groups. We can distinguish two particular research problems. The first is that of establishing the nature and extent of control possessed by different occupational groups and the second is that of analysing how control is affected when job structures change.

In examining the control that people have, however, it is essential to take into consideration accountability. Changes in organizational forms can have major impacts on the range of responsibility and extent of discretion within each area of responsibility as to how to perform a job; some changes which increase responsibility and discretion may also, at the same time, increase exposure to a more clearly articulated set of performance criteria (accountability).

Decentralization of the Personnel Function

Whilst the broader aspects of the personnel function, unlike the supply of training, cannot be externalized, their position in an organization can be altered. During the last decade, there have been trends towards decentralization with the reduction in multi-employer agreements but, at the level of the organization no such general movement can be observed in relation to pay or in establishing personnel policies and procedures. However, regarding recruitment and training, decisions are now more likely to be taken by the departmental or line managers concerned.

Supply Teaching and the Concept of Substitution

The term 'supply teacher' is somewhat ambiguous. At its broadest it may be used to represent those without a normal or 'regular' contract of employment, i.e., all non-full-time and non-permanent teachers employed in the education system at any particular moment or during a survey reference period. Regular part-timers and temporary full-timers on long-term contracts are then grouped together with temporary staff on short-term contracts (sometimes a succession of contracts with the same employer if not the same school) and temporary staff employed at such short notice and for such a short period that they correspond more to a form of casual worker. Regular part-time teachers appear to straddle the boundary between fully integrated regular full-timers and the more marginal temporary employees.

The associations between these constituents vary in strength according to the aspect of the employment relationship and teaching outcome being considered. For presentational purposes in reports dealing with teacher supply, it may be convenient to group them together; for analytical purposes it is both unnecessary and undesirable (Great Britain Parliament, House of Commons, 1990, 1991; Galloway, 1993). Looked at from the demand side (schools/LEAs) or supply side (teachers), these categories reflect contractual outcomes which are significantly different and changes in the pattern of employment contracts are often symptomatic of deeper shifts in the organizations concerned. Moreover, the qualitative nature of the teacher's work differs both between and within categories depending on the school or department within a school; witness the different degrees to which non-regular staff are involved in curriculum development, planning of the work, and pupil assessment as opposed to class teaching. It appears that the functions being carried out by non-regular teachers can actually be quite different from those of the regular teacher. This may, of course, be a consequence of time-scale since short supply periods hardly provide scope for engaging in all aspects of the professional role. But other factors are also important and these are explored by Galloway (1991b) and those authors cited by her.

Robert M. Lindley

The above, however, focuses only on the external labour market conception of 'supply' where recruitment takes place. A clearer functional conception of supply would also include internal labour market adjustments where cover is provided by regular staff already employed. This is achieved by substituting class teaching for non-teaching time and allowing the potential shortage of staff for one task, namely teaching, to be transformed into a shortage of staff time in another task, e.g., curriculum development or school management. Again, depending on the individuals concerned, the teaching role performed in the given area of cover may be much more limited than that performed by the regular teacher. Combining classes or re-distributing pupils among other classes involves not just a substitution among the staff inputs to the class teaching function but a restructuring of the function itself as represented by the task of teaching larger classes, etc.

Taken a step further, the concept of 'supply teaching' involving a narrower professional role may be extended to include subjects being taught through non-subject specialists, whether as regular or supply teachers — in a pejorative term, a form of 'subject-minding' by analogy with 'child-minding'.

Thus the notion of supplying some teaching to fill a gap while proper arrangements can be made should not be confined to the practice of employing people on temporary contracts. Recourse to supply teaching, in that sense, may describe all strategies used to substitute existing or new personnel for the person regularly employed to do a particular job or for the sort of person whom the employer would like to recruit to fill the job on a regular basis. However, a particular supply teacher (internally or externally provided) might fall into the category of acceptable candidate for a regular post but might not be willing to work on a regular basis. Even in the case of such a supply teacher, substitution is unlikely to be perfect because the short-run circumstances will normally make this infeasible.

Analysis of supply teaching must then take account of the qualitative differences in personnel employed as substitutes and the qualitative outcome for the educational process. But the latter is not merely a function of the former. Supply situations may lead to a conscious or unconscious redesigning of the job which is over and above that dictated by the logistics of the situation. Increasing attention is being paid to the relative contribution of supply teacher, the regular teacher for whom cover is being arranged, and school policy in determining changes in the job carried out.

Galloway (1991a), however, makes a further point. Supply situations should not be assumed inevitably to force an impoverished professional role upon the teacher which, when reinforced by the effects of disruption, leads to a lowering of educational quality experienced by the pupil. More positive outcomes which involve working with the particular supply teacher's skills and experience and fostering the potential educational value of *discontinuity* should also be recognized even if, in current practice, they are rare.

The Structuring of the Supply 'Problem'

Educational Change and School Occupational Structures

Widespread changes in the education system have been introduced relatively quickly in ways which have deprived a large system of opportunities to benefit from careful experimentation and the economies of scale potentially available to it (especially in terms of the research, design and development of new curricula, delivery methods, assessment and staff training).

Moreover, the organization of the system has been decentralized such that all its components (LEAs and schools) were having to learn together to tackle basic problems of interpreting the aims and regulations of reform, planning and implementation, with insufficient opportunity to benefit from other parts of the system being further up the 'learning curve'.

Yet in terms of being an employing organization, the school appears to have emerged from a period of diminished responsibility. This has involved a certain amount of cultural shock. For example, schools complain about the need to take into account financial considerations when appointing teachers. It has been of special concern to those schools which have a disproportionately high number of experienced teachers and must adopt a policy of recruiting younger teachers when older teachers leave or supply cover is required in order to reduce staff costs to bring expenditure in line with LMS budgets.

But this also has a systemic effect. If schools have no strong incentive to consider the trade-off between employing experienced as opposed to inexperienced teachers and LEAs prove ineffectual in maintaining parity among schools, this will also tend to polarize schools into those able to attract and retain the most able and experienced teachers and those continually struggling to recruit adequate staff.

In effect, the greater budgetary freedom now given to schools means that they face trade-offs between choices which were not previously linked at all or not so directly. Although the removal of a constraint will not affect behaviour unless it was previously a binding constraint, it is likely that some schools at least will take the freedom to substitute one form of expenditure for another. This recognition of trade-offs in a context of having real power to save in one area and spend in another is undoubtedly still viewed as a mixed blessing. It will, however, no more turn a school into a cost-minimizing organization than into a profit-maximizer (Keep, 1993a). What we would expect to happen, nonetheless, is a progressive adjustment of the cost-structure of the school up to the point at which the distortions created by the traditionally extensive DES/LEA direction of funding according to category of spending are removed.

The balance of expenditure between broad categories such as investment in new buildings, equipment, maintenance or books and staffing is thus likely to change quite independently of the changes in pressures to which schools are being subjected, simply because the previous balance was not the choice of the same group of actors in the system; so, also, could the balance of expenditure within categories.

What is perhaps surprising and a testament to professional control is the rather rigid way in which LEAs operated as employers in the pre-reform period. Teachers were allocated to subjects and schools with little recourse to system-wide flexibility except in periods of re-deployment following rationalization such as comprehensivization or adaptation to major demographic change. Most LEAs did little to develop personnel strategies which as a matter of routine sought to place the interests of the system as a whole above those of individual schools; when they did so, it was usually belated (DES, 1990). Admittedly during the 1980s LEAs began to behave more strategically, arguably starting to catch up on modes of personnel planning and practice which had reached other parts of the local authority sector and private business. It is, however, ironic that this took place at a time when the government was beginning to emasculate the LEA as an employer and that the final flush of LEA activity on the personnel-policy front involved authority-wide training initiatives, funded by the DES, designed to cope with a multitude of educational reforms of which one was the very measure, delegation to schools and governing bodies, which would call into question the LEA's role as employer in the future (Leighton, 1990).

The fact that there were so many schools in attractive areas of some LEAs with salary costs well above those indicated by formula funding is as much evidence of the failure of the previous employment policy to allocate resources in accordance with need as of failure of the new policy to allow adequately for the circumstances of different schools. Even where there are arrangements for a modification of the funding formula for a transitional period, school heads and governors continue to complain about the underlying rationale of the system.

Part of the problem, of course, is that the new financial system is being introduced in a very restrictive budgetary climate and teachers threatened by, and weary of, reforms may perhaps be forgiven for confusing the effects of the new system with the effects of financial stringency overall. Part of the problem is also that the education system lacks the national human resources framework which its complexity requires (Keep, 1993b) and within which LEAs could operate.

The Social Construction of Skill and Professional Functions

An implication of research on occupational and organizational change is that the social construction of skills is a reality which should be recognized by all participants in the labour market. This is especially marked in highly regulated areas involving professional labour markets.

All professional groups try to demarcate their areas of control and seek to avoid notions of substitutability between tasks to be carried out by them and other occupations; this might lead to progressive substitution of people trained in another tradition for their own members. Even substitution at the margin is seen as potentially damaging. This is inevitable: every occupational group with opportunities based on high levels of the relatively scarce skills involved or on industrial bargaining strength will seek to exercise that power in their own interests.

In order to achieve this situation professions seek to promote notions that:

- there is a unity of interest between themselves and the consumers of the services they provide;
- the qualifications and experiences of the professionals make them ideally placed to determine what is in the best interests of the community regarding the definition and delivery of the service;
- these same professional characteristics make the professional bodies the best judge of what qualifications should be required of those allowed to deliver the service;
- the State, recognizing the points above, should ensure that the provision of the service should be regulated by the profession within a framework of law; and

- in the case of publicly-funded professional activities, the government should take responsibility, because of its overall responsibility for the funding of the service, when the professional bodies or their members make mistakes but should have the minimum control over the conduct of the process by which the professional service is defined, delivered, priced and marketed.

The first item is crucially important. The professions thus try to build and sustain a belief in the professional and consumer interests being indivisible. Part of this process involves establishing a professional culture in which it is virtually seen as being offensive to suggest that there is a difference between the interests of professionals and consumers. It is argued that the key divergence is between the interests of different consumers: resources given to one cannot be given to another. The professional is taxed with the responsibility of pursuing an equitable allocation between competing groups, often having to make invidious decisions.

Whilst the above objectives do relate to the teaching profession, it has been much less successful than lawyers and doctors in achieving them. In the two last points above, respectively, teachers have either never had the regulatory power given to the other two groups or have struggled to maintain footholds, and have not managed to divert criticism quite so deftly to the government of the day.

Continuing Training: Market or Non-market Situations?

The problem of supply cover has been raised particularly in relation to the training needs of regular staff (Brown and Earley, 1990). Increased training activity consequent on educational reform (of which one reform was itself concerned with the provision of continuing training) has generated an increased need for temporary cover. The implications of this for the longer term do, however, depend on the extent to which the transition is to a new relatively stable system with less traumatic adjustments in prospect or to a system characterized by continuous change over the foreseeable future. In the former case the dislocation created between the demands of the covered jobs and the skills and experience of the supply teacher will be removed — almost all supply teachers have been established teachers. New cohorts of supply teachers will have had the necessary training; older cohorts may with a little help make the necessary adjustments.

In the latter case of dynamic change, where the supply teacher body is continually behind in adjusting to the needs of the jobs to be covered, two things can happen: the job can be temporarily de-skilled sufficiently for the supply teacher to cope with it or the quality of the service to the pupil can be lowered temporarily.

The supply teacher can be so closely programmed that the pupil's education is not affected in the short-term or can be allowed to follow a less demanding schedule on the assumption that ground can be made up by the regular teacher later. The supply teacher operating the educational machinery on automatic pilot or acting as child-minder/occupier/ entertainer are two extremes with deeper implications; they provide threatening images which the profession rejects as infeasible in the first case and wholly unacceptable in the second case.

For if supply teachers can be 'programmed' so might teaching assistants and other ancillary staff (technicians, library assistants, trainees, school administrators/secretaries). The range of choice of occupational structure for a school and the contractual options entertained then appear to be rather wider than would first appear. Effecting a new division of labour between professionals and existing or new groups of intermediate professionals, taking advantage of progressively more appropriate educational technology, would alter the method of organizational adjustment to expected or unexpected requirements for cover. Supply strategies then become open to revision for it may be possible to select occupational structures which help to reduce the effects of fluctuations in the number of regular teachers available.

However, supply teachers complain not so much of being unable to cope because they need to be updated professionally; they are more inclined to complain about their existing skills not being fully used in supply situations. The form of complaint is that they are deprived of sufficient information about what is required of them and about the framework within which they will be working (Shilling, 1991a).

Arguably, the explicitness and transparency of curriculum aims and the availability of better teaching material under the new system should improve the situation because supply teachers will have available much better information with which to orientate themselves and more professional teaching aids.

At this point, the problem of supply cover meets that of teacher shortage. Occupational structures which tackle the former may also ameliorate the latter. But the two are, nonetheless, quite different. In the first case, part of the problem is its unexpectedness and/or temporary nature whereas, in the second case, it is the persistence of the problem which renders it largely predictable. The fact that a large excess supply of all types of teachers would solve both problems does not add to our understanding of either. Where they meet is in relation to training and it is here where the problem of supply cover does shed light on the shortages issue.

Internalization/Externalization in the INSET Field

The implication of the above for supply teaching is that the more developed the training market is the more accessible training will be for the individual who, through preference or necessity does not have a stable employment relationship or for those regular employees who cannot persuade an employer to provide the training they want to have. The market structure is then in place through which to equip members of the teaching force with the appropriate training. However, the right market signals need to be sent for this to lead to a diminution in shortages whether of supply teachers or regular teachers in shortage subjects and/or in unattractive employment environments. The cost of courses, their curricula, methods of delivery and scheduling, together with the perceived benefits they have for participants will influence take-up.

Learning from the Margin of the Profession

So, as a labour market phenomenon, we have observed supply teachers in a period of intensive educational reform, marked by the need for greater continuing training of existing teachers and by financial stringency and uncertainty facing their immediate (schools) and proximate employers (LEAs).

Yet as a matter of research strategy much can be learnt about the professions and their labour markets, even when not faced with great change, by examining the conditions under which some employees, despite their qualifications and experience are engaged under marginal contracts if not in marginal capacities. The functions they perform, their positions relative to fellow professionals and to other occupational groups can reveal aspects of the underlying nature of the labour market concerned which are obscured by focusing only on the mainstream.

Attempts by trade unions or professional associations to limit the size of the margin and by employers to increase it tend to obscure the fact that both benefit from it. Uncertainties and the extent of curtailed opportunities facing 'regular members' of the profession can be reduced by concentrating their effects on marginal members. The latter buttress the positions of the former by providing them with greater job security, training and promotion opportunities because their own can be sacrificed by the employer when financial imperatives must be faced.

For a profession losing its grip on the process of educational change and on the nature of the employment relationship within education, it is all the more convenient to have a natural pool of professionally committed but dispensable members, people who will stand in for the regular teacher when illness, training, or other duties take them away from the classroom; people whose situations leave them with little power to protest at neglect by either their professional colleagues or their employers (see, for example, Trotter and Wragg, 1990).

But we are not talking of poorly qualified, inexperienced, or less competent teachers; all occupations have such groups. In the case of education, more than most, our concern is with experienced, well-qualified, highly competent teachers (Eyles, 1992). This poses problems both for the trade unions and employers in dealing with the conflicts between interest, equity and efficiency. Trade unions experience conflict between, especially, the first two of these and employers between the last two. To what extent can different labour market structures resolve both of these conflicts? In particular, could the pursuit of equity be compatible with the interests of the majority of teachers and with the pursuit of efficiency by employers?

It is worth noting that the focus here is not on supply teachers *per se* but on supply teaching. The majority of supply teachers are women returners most of whom will eventually obtain regular employment, though often on a part-time basis. The process of supply is a phase in the occupational re-integration of professional women as well as a short-term recruitment and deployment option used by employers faced with unexpected and/or temporary staff needs (Morrison, 1991). How far can the 'phase'-'option' perspectives be reconciled? Is it possible to transform 'supply' from a stage in the downward mobility initially experienced by so many women returning to careers after a break?

There are really three alternative objectives:

- improve efficiency in terms of the provision of supply cover in response to the way demand emerges from the current system;
- re-assess the occupational structure of schools, taking into account the need for teacher substitution by both qualified teachers and other groups, so as to reduce the need for marginal supply posts; and

Robert M. Lindley

- look at supply cover in terms of the long-term recruitment and retention of women teachers.

The first approach is essentially concerned with improving efficiency within the existing system, accepting the limited room for manœuvre of schools which must work within poorly articulated personnel policies at LEA and national level and the mix of incentives currently available. The second is concerned with achieving greater effectiveness in teacher deployment and substitution by facing the threats and opportunities attached to experimenting with more flexible occupational structures and a re-definition of the relative roles of school, LEA and national authority. The third is concerned with the extent to which pursuing greater equity in the treatment of women members of the profession will also yield benefits under the efficiency/effectiveness heading.

It would seem that limiting objectives to the first and second elements will not meet the needs of the system or of a majority of women teachers. The ramifications of confining reform to creating more efficient markets for supply teachers with little effective widening of the scope for substitution are likely to be considerable: current pay structures, modes of training provision, occupational patterns, and funding structures all sustain the under-utilization of women trained as teachers. Pay structures on the one hand give women returners salaries which are too high, from the point of view of school budgets, compared with cheaper younger teachers and too low, when combined with other conditions of employment, to attract enough women qualified in shortage subjects back to the profession (Shilling, 1990, 1991b).

Training provision concentrates on initial teacher training for young adults with 40 per cent wastage after four years followed by forms of in-service training to which access is mainly obtained by having a teaching job. Funding structures fail to link, at the level of the educational employer (LEA/school), the costs of initial training with the pay differential between younger and older teachers, so savings on the former by greater utilization of those already trained cannot be seen to compensate for the latter. Nor can the former be seen by schools as their investment which launches the individual teacher into a profile of rising productivity, the benefits of which are felt by the school in the higher quality of education it provides, as training and experience interact, and by the teacher through higher pay and job satisfaction.

Yet these considerations yield more radical implications for what constitutes good teaching and the training and experience which most effectively fosters it. The relationships between function, qualification and occupation must be seen not only in terms of 'system' but also 'working life', not only in terms which preoccupy organizations but also those which are meaningful to individuals. At present the discontinuity between these perceptions arises through different values placed on a particular form of experience: motherhood.

Conclusion

The developments in British education thus exhibit functional relocation, the creation of markets where they did not exist, shifting of organization — market boundaries, externalization and internalization of particular functions, and substantial pressure to reconsider if not reform the job content and occupational structures of schools. But all these changes are taking place in a context in which the formal employing organization (LEA) is being forced to divest itself of much of the power which characterizes such an organization.

In corporate terms, the head office (LEA) is required:

- to create independent divisions (schools) providing similar products and competing with each other in the interests of the consumer; and
- to subject itself to competition from other potential suppliers of the functions it has hitherto performed for the divisions, in the interests of raising the quality and lowering the cost of its central services.

The emasculation of the 'corporation' as an employing organization is accompanied by the imposition of a regulatory role which involves monitoring the performance of the divisions and transmitting information about their performance to consumers and shareholders (the government and community at large). The analogy, like all analogies, will break down if pushed too far but the principal elements are valid.

In effect, the LEA is apparently being transformed into the kind of organization least likely to provide high-quality jobs and continuing training: a constellation of small enterprises operating under severe financial pressure in a market of mounting competition, with an unpredictable bank manager, and a supplier of major services (the LEA) facing major uncertainty as to its continuing viability.

In this climate, the experimentation with different models of training and supply teaching which is already apparent will undoubtedly continue. Particularly important will be the initiative shown by LEAs in creating a framework which helps to promote collective efficiency and risk-sharing among schools.

The basic elements of the framework would include:

- promoting a more developed market for supply teachers with information accessible to teachers, schools and LEAs, perhaps involving compulsory registration with the authority for any qualified teacher wanting to teach but not currently employed on a regular full-time basis and in advance of applying for any post or responding to a request for emergency cover;
- promoting a market for training which is more independent of the teachers' labour market by supplying courses which are accessible to all with suitable qualifications, not just those currently in regular employment in the authority or elsewhere; and
- providing a risk-sharing insurance scheme for supply cover dealing with emergency supply relating to illness and other situations not under the control of the school.

Beyond this, however, the economics of LMS and DFE discretionary funding of LEAs in the areas of training raise a number of questions which need to be more clearly worked out. Many of these echo the dilemmas faced in other areas of the labour market.

The central issue, however, is the extent to which the education system with its constituent employing organizations attempts to provide women teachers with career structures that recognize the full range of their experience and avoid the barriers to maintaining continuity of career development across the full and partial career breaks relating to family formation and childcare.

Note

1 This chapter is based substantially on a paper of the same title presented to the 1991 BERA Annual Conference. I am grateful to Sheila Galloway, Marlene Morrison and other participants in the symposium on supply teaching in English schools for comments on that earlier draft and to Ms Galloway and Ms Morrison for their help and patience as editors of the present volume.

References

BROWN, S. and EARLEY, P. (1990) *Enabling Teachers to Undertake In-Service Education and Training*, HMSO/NFER.

CASEY, B. (1988) *Temporary Employment Practice and Policy in Britain*, London, Policy Studies Institute.
DES (1990) *Teacher Supply in Seventeen Schools in Tower Hamlets and Wandsworth*, A Report by HM Inspectorate 159/90/DS, London, DES.
EYLES, W. (1992) 'Job-Sharing and Other Forms of Flexible Working in Teaching: promoting the return to teaching of highly qualified staff', Unpublished report for the Department for Education.
GALLOWAY, S. (1991a) 'Demanding and Supplying: Senior Teachers' Perspectives on Supply', BERA Annual Conference, Nottingham Polytechnic, August.
GALLOWAY, S. (1991b) 'Demanding Supply: School Perspectives', CEDAR Seminar Paper, University of Warwick.
GALLOWAY, S. (1993) '"Out of Sight, Out of Mind": A response to the literature on supply teaching', *Educational Research*, 35, 2, pp. 159–69.
GRACE, G. and LAWN, M. (Eds) (1991) *Teacher Supply and Teacher Quality*, Clevedon, Multilingual Matters.
GREAT BRITAIN PARLIAMENT, HOUSE OF COMMONS (Interim Advisory Committee) (1990) *Third Report of the Interim Advisory Committee on School Teachers' Pay and Conditions, 30 January*, (Chairman: Lord Chilver), London, HMSO.
GREAT BRITAIN PARLIAMENT, HOUSE OF COMMONS (Interim Advisory Committee) (1991) *Fourth Report of the Interim Advisory Committee on School Teachers' Pay and Conditions, 18 January*, (Chairman: Lord Chilver), London, HMSO.
KEEP, E. (1993a) 'Schools in the Marketplace? — Some Problems with Private Sector Models', *Local Management of Schools': Bera Dialogues*, 6, Clevedon, Multilingual Matters, pp. 102–18.
KEEP, E. (1993b) 'The Need for a Revised Management System for the Teaching Profession', *Education Economics*, 1, 1, pp. 53–9.
LEIGHTON, P. (1990) 'Codification, Classification and Prescription in Teachers' Contracts', *Research in Education Management and Policy: Retrospect and Prospect*, SARAN, R. and TRAFFORD, V. (Eds), London, The Falmer Press, pp. 129–34.
LINDLEY, R.M. (1987) *New Forms and New Areas of Employment Growth: A Comparative Study*, Brussels, CEC.
LINDLEY, R.M. (1991a) 'Interactions in the Markets for Education, Training and Labour: A European Perspective on Intermediate Skills', *International Comparisons of Vocational Education and Training for Intermediate Skills*, RYAN, P. (Ed.), London, The Falmer Press, pp. 185–206.
LINDLEY, R.M. (1991b) 'Individuals, Human Resources and Markets', *Training and Competitiveness*, STEVENS, J. and MACKAY, C. (Eds), London, Kogan Page, pp. 201–28.
MILLWARD, N. and STEVENS, M. (1986) *British Workplace Industrial Relations 1980–1984*, Aldershot, Gower.
MILLWARD, N., STEVENS, M., SMART, D. and HAWES, W.R. (1992) *Workplace*

Industrial Relations in Transition, Aldershot, Dartmouth Publishing Company.
MORRISON, M. (1991) 'The Language of Supply: A Shifting Interface for LEAs, Schools and Supply Teachers', BERA Annual Conference, Nottingham Polytechnic, August.
RYAN, P. (1991) (Ed.) *International Comparisons of Vocational Education and Training for Intermediate Skills*, London, The Falmer Press.
SHILLING, C. (1990) 'The Organization of Supply Workers in State Schools and the National Health Service: a comparison', *Journal of Education Policy*, 5, 2, pp. 127–41.
SHILLING, C. (1991a) 'Supply Teachers: working on the margins: A review of the literature', in *Educational Research*, 33 1.
SHILLING, C. (1991b) 'Permanent Supports or Temporary Props? Supply Workers in State Schools and the National Health Service', in *Gender and Education*, 33 1.
STENNING, R. (1990) 'School Staff Employment Trends in the Maintained Sector: Some Agendas for Research', *Research in Education Management and Policy: Retrospect and Prospect*, SARAN, R. and TRAFFORD, V. (Eds), London, The Falmer Press, pp. 171–7.
TROTTER, A. and WRAGG, E. (1990) 'A study of supply teachers,' *Research Papers in Education*, 5, 3.

Chapter 11

Conclusion: Confronting Paradox

Sheila Galloway and Marlene Morrison

In Chapter 1 we suggested that there was more than one supply story and this poses prospects for diverse endings. For some participants in our research, as indeed for some readers, making visible the paradox of supply teaching signals both an ending to this book and a beginning. In this first full-length publication on supply teaching, the seemingly powerful yet powerless position of supply teachers has moved centre-stage as part of a wider arena in which a marginalized work-force underpins an educational system which has failed to recognize its contribution. Paradox has been revealed at other levels. Having acquired a peculiar status and security value for schools when they are unavailable or most urgently needed (Morrison, 1993), both the status and influence of supply teachers have been shown to decline at the point of school entry. Ambivalence is also apparent in the classroom where substitute teachers are expected to be simultaneously active and passive in their approach.

Diverse contributions have stressed distinct as well as overlapping issues of teacher substitution. Congruence between chapters has sometimes been partial; this is neither unexpected nor unintended. If boundaries need to be set this does not imply an immutable stance. We learn from diversity and unpredictability. Eclectism, however, does not preclude some preferences in our own approach. These are revealed in Chapter 1 and in others; they stem from our own research backgrounds, and interest in qualitative approaches to social investigation, as well as from personal experience.

Connections and Disconnections

Conclusions refocus our attention on some of the connections and disconnections, and, given the perspectives examined, suggest implications for educational practitioners and social scientists, who each have different priorities in seeking solutions and explanations. These are approached at four specific levels and through a number of educational themes.

The National Level

At the national level there has been a transient emphasis on supply teaching as aspects of overall teacher supply during a period of unprecedented teacher training. In a world that is now changing fundamentally for regular teachers in permanent posts, how much more this applies to supply teaching. Present trends are that the need for training for permanent staff will continue as successive phases of the National Curriculum are implemented. Supply teachers need to be professionally up-to-date as much as those they replace, and their working situations call for high classroom management skills. They have, however, no contractual relationship with LEA or school, and therefore no job security (except in the case of the very few remaining full-time team members retained by some LEAs, and part-time teachers who choose to work extra hours on a supply basis). Yet national policy has still to formulate a response. This leaves supply teachers in a kind of educational limbo, free to join an expanding group of freelance professionals who, like freelancers outside education, face opportunities and constraints. However, unlike educational professionals at more senior consultancy levels, they experience opportunities and constraints at the sharp end of school finance in which funding for teacher substitution may not be among the main priorities. In Chapter 10 we were reminded that such changes had factors in common with a number of highly qualified groups outside teaching.

The Local Level

A curtailed role for LEAs makes the notion of an integrated education service increasingly questionable. Several chapters have illustrated what is possible when LEAs have taken a pro-active stance on supply teaching issues, either through LEA-focused action or through providing supportive networks in which self-help groups and school-based initiatives can thrive. In the 1990s, responsibility for supply matters lies almost wholly with schools, and, for the first time, new entrants to the

Conclusion: Confronting Paradox

supply scene, namely private teacher agencies. Whether they will be able to fill the employment and training needs of schools and supply teachers respectively remains to be seen. Meanwhile in 1993 GEST funding for women returners ceased, such schemes being perceived as less of a priority once short-term shortages appeared to have eased. A longer term view is that this can only be a temporary respite.

Policy statements at national levels have highlighted the importance of retraining and effectively deploying supply staff. LEAs have been expected to respond simultaneously to top–down advice to tackle the supply situation, whilst attempting to meet the bottom–up demands for competent teachers. Yet a very basic level of involvement is now common-place in LEAs, although several authorities have advocated insurance policies to schools for short-term absence covered by LEAs and perhaps, in the future, by teacher agencies. Whilst LEAs continue to be involved in police vetting and administration, total levels of cover are apparent only at school level. Such developments confirm a continuing dependence on a peripheral work-force with contradicting tendencies towards integrating supply teachers and yet making them invisible at school and local levels. Whilst we have shown that the conflation of returners' and supply teachers' needs has raised the profile of both in some LEAs, this has not always helped to define the specific skills required of supply teachers.

The Institutional Level

If there is a proliferation of opinions about supply teaching, nowhere is this more apparent than at the level of the school. This volume has shown that it is possible to move beyond a basic discussion of supply issues in terms of availability to a more sensitive recognition of the complex issues relating to continuity and discontinuity in teaching and learning in schools. Several chapters have explored the early impact of budgetary decisions made in the context of local management of schools, and have also highlighted strategies to encourage more systematic use of supply cover. This includes the bedding down of new structures, and we are reminded that the temptation (necessity even) to save and vire monies from the supply budget is great, especially in small schools. This is the arena in which macro-level initiatives, directives, and decisions are shown to intersect at the micro-level with school priorities and the day-to-day impact of teacher absence and disturbance to routine.

The Individual Level

Supply teachers appear to be as diverse as teachers in regular employment in terms of educational philosophy, training, teaching skills, and subject knowledge. As we have shown, this range is complicated by their various reasons for working on an occasional basis, wide variations in their levels of employment, and an absence of school-based identity and membership. An understanding of supply teacher identities has been a central feature of one chapter together with a rare acknowledgment and celebration of out-of-school knowledge and career break experience in another. The importance of grass-roots activity among a small group of supply teachers has also been discussed.

The overwhelming weight of evidence is that supply teaching is held by all parties to have little status. Yet for potential returners to teaching, supply experiences can be critical in deciding whether to return or not. We juxtaposed the sometimes contradictory expectations of supply teachers to examine the images which have predominated and the way supply teacher identities are sustained.

At each of these levels, issues remain critical for schools, pupils, and teachers alike. What signs are there of possible future directions and what suggestions can be made for ways forward?

Ways Forward

We have already sounded warning signals about cost-cutting measures in some schools. In the absence of national and local impetus, other schools experiment with small-scale support for supply staff. The development of private agencies, or new variants on LEA supply teacher agencies, introduces other possibilities for training and professional development, although in a increasingly heterogeneous educational market, we have yet to see what precisely their role will be.

At national level, the evidence indicates a lack of policy about training and managing a substitute teaching force. Among the minimum ways forward are: first, that, at national level, recognition is needed that substitute teachers are qualified professionals; second, that better quantitative information is required nationally about numbers of supply teachers; third, that encouragement could be given to exploring flexible forms of work in teaching; and fourth, that central funding is required to support training that directly tackles the particular needs of supply teachers.

Conclusion: Confronting Paradox

At local levels, the curtailed role of LEAs means that most aspects of supply provision are now devolved to schools. In current circumstances, where LEAs can only justify expenditure on priorities, there are, perhaps, the least grounds for optimism. Nevertheless, evidence from the research and our various contributions leads us to conclude that the following are minimum requirements. Regional collaboration is needed between authorities so that vetting of teachers who move from one area to another occurs speedily, thus eliminating delay in employing suitable staff who have not yet been cleared by a previous employer. A reliable database held centrally by an LEA, and regularly updated, can enable supply teachers and schools to be 'matched'. In some authorities this is better operated at a district level, or through 'clusters' of schools. Arrangements could be made for supply teachers to join other training sessions provided by LEAs. Designated LEA representatives could coordinate information for supply teachers, and act as liaison with all supply staff. For those working occasionally, contact points and information networks are critical. Chapter 10 again pinpointed the frameworks that LEAs can offer in promoting collective efficiency and risk-sharing among schools.

At institutional level, we have examined examples of schools which are developing mechanisms to manage cover of classes under current budgetary constraints. Some level of teacher absence is endemic to schools as organizations, and a proportion of this can be foreseen, with an element allowed for unpredictable or short-term absence. The balance between internal and external cover is critical. Does it benefit primary pupils for the headteacher to cover classes? In the secondary phase, how might one juxtapose questions of specialist competence as against general teaching skills, and still minimize the likelihood of *ad hoc* judgments? In any school, communication between the supply teacher and the regular teacher is critical. Monitoring reasons for teacher absence from classes would encourage continuity for pupils. A supply teacher in a primary or secondary classroom needs essential information. Recognizing the time spent on managing supply situations, an allocation of non-contact time for the teacher organizing supply cover appears to us essential. Whole-school awareness of the need for training and professional development for supply teachers alongside permanent staff would be a positive move; as yet there is little evidence of this.

When women predominate numerically, the supply teacher can be said to typify the socio-economic features of a gendered profession even more markedly than the teachers in full-time employment. Yet the evidence does not entirely confirm the stereotype. Supply work is seen variously by supply teachers as a personal 'keeping in touch' programme, a step towards returning to teaching, or a post-retirement link with the profession. For some it is a financial safety net but for others, the essential family income. We have illustrated that supply teaching calls for many professional skills, and that this expertise is extended in different schools and situations, but offers few career prospects and few opportunities for training. Among the difficulties in understanding teaching is a failure to give due emphasis to the temporal constraints underpinning current forms of mass schooling. Such issues are critically focused in substitute teaching. More basic research is needed on teaching and learning processes which could help both regular and supply teachers determine priorities in providing substitution. To date many individual supply teachers have taken the initiative in approaching local schools, and in developing home-based resource banks from which they draw at short notice. Supply teachers need training and professional development tailored to the needs of the job, and access to training opportunities for regular staff in local schools.

Conceptual Bridges

In Chapter 1 we highlighted some conceptual links underpinning the analysis of supply teaching and located the various contributions of this volume along the spectrum of identified themes. Here, Lukes' (1974) analysis of power relations offers sensitizing concepts (Hammersley and Atkinson, 1983); in particular, his 'third dimension' encourages us to consider what supply teachers are doing when they are or are not working in schools, whilst giving parallel attention to a gendered occupation in which issues of time, career, and professionalism are also prominent. For researchers, the study of predictable and unpredictable phenomena posed and poses continuing methodological challenges. (Morrison and Galloway, 1993; Galloway, 1992b).

Future significance for social scientists attaches to key aspects identified in the volume. Among outcomes are those which direct our attention towards developing further understandings about the relationship between educational policy and practice. The study of teacher substitution also takes us to the heart of the sociology of teaching and learning. Further recognition of discontinuous and irregular teaching will require that more attention be given to the constituent features of 'ordinary' teaching and learning. This is particularly significant in current contexts where understandings about such processes are undergoing reinterpretation and reassessment. The aim to track assumptions about supply teaching at meso- and micro-levels has meant assessing systems, structures, and interactions at four specific yet inter-connected levels. Power relations shaping supply teaching impinge on many areas of educational life; linking empirical findings with the abstract facilitates ways of exploring the issues further. Contributions to this volume have supported existing analysis of women's employment experience. However, they also warn against oversimplification in the links between gender and occupation, employment choice and necessity, core and periphery, and point to distinctions between the needs of women returners and those of supply teachers.

Professionalism Re-assessed

Contributors have challenged the commonly voiced view of supply teaching as 'just baby-sitting' and assert their role as professionals alongside permanent staff. Academic subject knowledge and general teaching skills are professional requirements of substitutes as much as of permanent staff. The name 'baby-sitters' implies lack of contact with pupils and a situation where pupils work on set exercises but no real learning occurs. Such occasions happen, both with internal cover by colleagues and with external supply staff (and on occasion, with regular teachers), but the evidence presented does not identify a marked tendency for supply teachers to avoid taking an active role.

There are spatial, temporal, and social implications in the balance of private and professional worlds. Whilst teacher substitutes are a heterogeneous group in terms of background, motives, and experience, a common thread is the juxtaposition of personal and professional commitments and time, frequently at very short notice. Issues in balancing private and public worlds remain complex, and part of another story that waits to be told.

Berg (1989, p. 58) notes that 'the basic condition of professionalization is that it must be sanctioned by the environment in which it is carried on'. In order to be sanctioned, supply teaching needs to be made visible along with other aspects of teaching and learning. This volume takes first steps in that direction. For employing organizations visibility includes recognition of the need to break down barriers and to reassess the value of career breaks. The contributions to this volume indicate that aspects of the professional world deserve reassessment by practitioners and researchers.

References

BERG, G. (1989) 'Educational reform and teacher professionalism', in *Journal of Curriculum Studies*, 21 1, pp. 53-60.
GALLOWAY, S. (1992b) 'Investigating The Irregular And The Unpredictable: reflections on research on supply teaching,', Paper presented at the St Hilda's Ethnography Conference, University of Warwick, September.
HAMMERSLEY, M. and ATKINSON, P. (1983) *Ethnography: Principles in Practice*, London, Tavistock Publications.
LUKES, S. (1974) *Power: A Radical View*, London, Macmillan.
MORRISON, M. (1993) 'Running for Cover: Substitute teaching and the secondary curriculum', in *Curriculum*, 14, 2, pp. 125-39.
MORRISON, M. and GALLOWAY, S. (1993) 'Researching Moving Targets: using diaries to explore supply teachers' lives', Paper presented at the British Sociological Association Conference, University of Essex, 5-8 April to be published in the selection of conference papers.

Appendix 1

Buckinghamshire Supply Teaching Questionnaire

The questionnaire (see Chapter 3) took most respondents an average of one hour to complete and the six sections were as follows:

Section A   Supply Teaching

- likes and dislikes about the work
- supply-teacher status (included because of responses in the pilot survey)
- views on cluster supply teaching (Cluster supply teaching in Milton Keynes meant a full or part-time supply teacher working on a 'permanent' contract with a small group of schools, who worked by flexible arrangement in those schools, one of which was the supply teacher's base.)
- suggestions for improving the quality of supply teaching
- views on the full-time permanent supply teacher 'pool'

Section B   Special issues for teachers new to supply teaching work

- induction?
- retraining?
- views on Milton Keynes booklet 'Guide to Primary Supply Teaching'

Section C   INSET (other than school-based or school-centred)

- INSET about supply teaching itself
- ideas for possible course content

Section D   Child-care provision

- whether this would help supply teachers work more frequently
- Any limiting factors?

Appendixes

Section E   Professional support other than INSET

- supply teacher practice in schools
- need for base for supply teachers with resources?

Section F   Personal details

- to establish distribution between sex and age group of participants
- professional training and experience
- family size, *re* nursery question
- current thoughts on career direction
- views on job-share

Methodology

Questions: these were posed in a variety of ways — multiple choice and multiple choice with a request to prioritize responses. There were open-ended and closed questions.

Confidentiality: surveys were identified only by the area of return e.g., AV for Aylesbury Vale, MK etc. This was marked on each survey as appropriate when it was sent out and then a number 001 etc. was added as they were returned. Participants could identify themselves if they wished.

Selection: the sample for Aylesbury Vale, Wycombe, Chiltern/South Bucks used the relevant supply lists, taking one in seven names and checking to ensure that a good geographical spread was achieved and a variety of infant/junior, first/middle preferences for work was covered. There was an attempt to achieve a balance between teachers who were prepared to work at short notice for short periods of time and those who would take on longer commitments. (This information is included for each supply teacher on the supply lists which go to schools).

Conclusions and Recommendations of the Research (Mullett, 1986)

The Work and Role of the Supply Teacher

1.1   Flexibility is the key factor which attracts teachers to supply work. Being made welcome is by far the most important reason for

Appendixes

accepting work in those schools. 58 per cent have worked in some schools where they found no welcome and no support.

1.2 Supply teachers try to continue the work of the class or provide parallel work which is stimulating. They need access to school resources.

1.3 To improve the service to schools they would like more information briefly over the telephone about the class they are to teach.

1.4 Cluster supply work does not appeal to about half the respondents because it entails reduced flexibility of working: those in favour (half) relish the opportunity to know children and staff better, see progress with the children and to 'belong'.

Issues for New Supply Teachers

2.1 73 per cent felt there should be a planned induction programme specifically about the specialism of supply teaching.

2.2 Re-training between first and middle school was also requested to reflect the fact that teaching is required across the entire primary age range.

2.3 Re-training from secondary to primary is also a factor.

2.4 The support group guide had been found helpful.

INSET other than School-based or School-centred

3.1 National Curriculum training is the over-riding need.

3.2 Planning work specifically for the supply situation and training in classroom organization for supply work are the two top priorities. Nearly half also wanted help on 'managing a group/behavioural issues'.

3.3 No clear preference emerged on the timing of INSET after school hours.

Child-care Provision

4.1 Nursery provision and post-5 after-school provision would theoretically help supply teachers to work more frequently.

4.2 School-based provision for the post-5 group was suggested. However, concern over the location of nursery provision and travelling times involved might reduce uptake.

Appendixes

4.3 It was suggested that supply teacher/full-time teacher use of child-care provision could be integrated with child-care provision for other workers.

Professional Support other than INSET

5.1 Information about each school on one sheet of paper given to every supply teacher on arrival at school is the most needed support. Half the responses also wanted active permission to use the school's resources.
5.2 There is a high commitment to provide a professional service to schools from those who answered this survey.
5.3 Distinction is made between 'one-off days' in schools, and extended periods of supply, in the latter case hoping to work like 'a full member of staff'.
5.4 Nowhere in this section was there awareness of the specific legal implications of the National Curriculum for classroom practice. This was picked up in other sections, however.
5.5 All but three supply teachers would use a base for supply teachers. They wanted most of all specific ideas for short-term supply work and social and professional contact with their peers.
5.6 Contact with advisers and other professionals within the Education Service would also be valued.

Personal Details

6.1 Most supply teachers are women.
6.2 Their date of qualifying as teachers range from 1953–1986. The varied age-groupings they trained for and have taught reflect changes in educational theory over those thirty-five years.
6.3 71 per cent have four or more years full-time experience which is an under-valued resource.
6.4 77 per cent have no clear plan to return to full-time teaching. They were in the process of deciding while 'on supply'. Their experiences on supply could influence their decision.
6.5 Job-share was seen as a way back to permanent posts by over half the respondents to the questionnaire. Those not interested are needed to provide the necessary flexibility to address the varying demands on the supply service.

Appendixes

Final Statement

Supply teachers are in a pivotal phase in their careers. They are learning to balance commitments outside teaching with their desire to serve the profession.

They may eventually take on more supply work, or return to full-time teaching, or not. Their decision will be based partly on non-teaching factors and partly on the warmth and quality of the welcome back they receive from their full-time professional colleagues.

Recommendations

Retention of Supply Teachers
1 Schools need to create a positive atmosphere for welcoming and supporting supply colleagues. Resources should be actively offered.
2 INSET is needed on the National Curriculum and its implication for supply teachers.
3 Induction and continuing INSET is needed on the specialism which is primary supply teaching.
4 A base for supply teachers in each area should be established with the facilities detailed in the survey results.
5 Opportunities for professional and social contact between supply teachers should be available.

Recruitment of Supply Teachers
6 Some information about the supply service and resources for teachers wishing to return to service after a career break should be available in local libraries.
7 A rolling series of brief advertisements in the local press should advertise the supply resource base, its meetings and 'drop in' times.

Appendix 2

Mandeville School Staff Cover Policy (see Chapter 5)

Within the context of the requirements of the 'Conditions of Service for Teachers in England and Wales' and as a result of full staff consultation, the following cover policy has been made.

1. Staff will continue to cover for a full 55/60 minute period.
2. As a general rule, sixth-form timetabled lessons will be covered.
3. Heads of year and newly qualified teachers will be given 'low priority' for cover.
4. The maximum number of planned absences during any one day will *normally* be 2.
5. If supply staff are funded but unavailable a course will be cancelled if reasonable notice can be given to the member of staff concerned.
6. The reasons for staff absence will be indicated on the cover slip. The following initials will be used:
    - A = Appointment
    - I = Illness
    - J = Journey/school vis't or trip
    - M = Meeting
    - P = Personal
    - T = Training
    - O = Appraisal observation

    The cover slip will also indicate as precisely as possible which parts of the day a member of staff is absent, when absence is for less than a whole day.
7. A teacher who is unexpectedly absent will normally phone work in. S/he will ensure that it is practicable, easily communicated, and appropriate to the length of lesson.
8. In addition, departments and years will maintain and issue 'banks' of work suitable for cover purposes.
9. Classes relocated for cover purposes will normally go into a classroom or equivalent, and not an open area such as the dining hall.

Appendixes

10 The school will continue to maintain open, summary records of cover done by staff.
11 Supply staff will normally be employed from the fourth day of absence (i.e., in line with Teachers' Conditions of Service); but where unusually difficult circumstances arise, this constraint may be disapplied at the discretion of the headteacher.
12 This cover policy will take immediate effect; and normally be reviewed annually, commencing a year from now.

Mandeville School *March 1993*

Notes on Contributors

Pauline Buzzing devised and ran the 'Keeping in Touch with Teaching' scheme for West Sussex LEA. She is now a freelance writer, trainer and consultant on education and author of two distance learning packs for returners and supply teachers: *An Effective return to Secondary Teaching* and *A Confident Return to Primary Teaching*.

Sheila Galloway is a research fellow in the Centre for Educational Development, Appraisal and Research at the University of Warwick. Originally a teacher of English, she later did comparative research on sociological aspects of vocational training in England and France. She has conducted research and published on teachers' in-service training and supply teaching. She is a joint author of *Implementing In-Service Education and Training* (1993).

Kath Green is a lecturer at Nottingham Trent University where she has led courses for both supply teachers and returners. Her interests include maths, education, gender issues, and parental involvement.

Cynthia Knight is headteacher of an infants' school in Birmingham, and was previously an LEA advisory teacher on the ORACY project. She has published on multicultural issues.

Robert Lindley is director of the Institute for Employment Research and professor at the University of Warwick. His main research as a labour market economist deals with patterns of economic and social change under different product and labour market conditions. Recent publications have included *Women's Employment: Britain in the Single European Market* (1992).

Marlene Morrison is a research fellow in the Centre for Educational Development and Research at the University of Warwick. She has lectured in further education, and did a study of part-time women students and lecturers in FE. Her research has included in-service training, school development plans, supply teaching, school library use, and, currently, teaching and learning about food and nutrition in schools. She is a joint author of *Implementing In-Service Education and Training*.

Mary Mullett is an educational consultant, previously County Co-ordinator for 'Keeping in Touch with Teaching' in Buckinghamshire. Originally a secondary teacher, she worked as a supply teacher for six years following a career break. After the formation of the Supply Teachers' Voluntary Support Group, she completed a survey on primary supply teaching issues. She has been involved in training courses for returners to teaching.

Malcolm Newton is headteacher of a secondary school in Buckinghamshire. He was a teacher fellow at CEDAR, seconded by Buckinghamshire LEA to conduct an evaluation of INSET. He is a joint author of *Implementing In-service Education and Training*.

Index

accountability 135, 152, 153
advertisements 90, 92, 118, 119, 132, 193
adaptability 51, 61, 91, 93, 100, 116, 119, 128, 144
agencies 1, 4, 9, 10, 108, 109, 113, 114, 115, 120, 134, 183, 184
Alexander, R. 140, 155
Anonymous 129, 135, 155
Anonymity 92, 103, 100, 105
appraisal 73, 109, 135, 142, 194
Arkin, A. 11, 85, 106
assertiveness 132
Atkinson, J. 83, 86, 106, 153–54, 155, 186
availability 48, 53, 71, 73, 76, 80, 90–92, 115, 144, 147, 148, 149, 153, 183

'babysitting' 10, 55, 62, 130, 143, 148, 187
Baker, L. 140, 155
Ball, D. 45, 64
Ball, S.J. 7, 11
Barnes, J. 29, 30
Bassey, M. 85, 106
Becker, H. 29, 30
Berg, G. 187, 188
Berkshire Department of Education 132, 135
Birmingham LEA 108, 113, 115
Blackburne, L. 11, 85, 106
British Educational Research Association 178, 180

British Sociological Association 12, 107
Brown, S. 5, 11, 44, 64, 85, 106, 139, 142, 144, 154, 155, 172, 178
BTEC xii, 71
Buckinghamshire LEA 12, 33, 34, 35, 41, 189
Bucks Primary Forum 69
Burgess, R.G. viii, x, 2, 7, 11, 106, 154, 155
Buzzing, P. 9, 83, 124, 136, 145, 155, 196

C.S.E. 128
C.P.V.E. xii, 71
Campbell, R.J. 49, 64
career breaks ix, 6, 8, 10, 16, 17, 24, 26, 28, 40, 41, 46, 103–4, 114, 115, 122, 124, 145, 150, 175, 178, 184, 187, 192–3
career development vii, 5, 6, 103, 117, 119, 135, 145, 146, 178, 190, 192, 193
case study 5, 11, 46, 82, 84, 85
Casey, K. 138, 155
Casey, B. 160, 179
CEDAR viii, x, xii, 11, 63, 106, 148, 155
Centrelink LEA 44, 55, 58
checklists (*see* information for supply teachers)
Chessum, L. 129, 136, 146, 155
childcare allowances and provision 150, 189, 191, 192

Index

childminding 10, 75, 103, 116, 142, 168, 173
children's development 17, 18–21, 29
 influences upon 24
 needs 20
 perspectives 29–30
 play 23–24
classroom management x, 3, 48, 51, 54, 62, 75, 76, 88, 99, 100, 103, 105, 135, 140, 181, 182, 191
commitment 46, 53, 56, 73, 95, 96, 112, 139, 142, 146, 187, 192
COMPACT 71
compatibility (*see also* mismatch) 70, 75, 76, 80, 84, 95, 101, 104, 111, 114, 117, 118, 172
competence 9, 95, 101, 130, 142, 175
competition 53, 87, 113, 123, 177
confidence 8, 32, 46, 93, 98, 101, 103, 124, 125, 126, 129, 130, 135, 142, 145
Connor, J. 5, 11, 85, 106
continuity 1, 9, 38, 45, 52, 92, 94, 96, 98, 101, 103, 105, 106, 115, 145, 183, 191
Cooley, C. 45, 64
community involvement 104, 109
core and periphery 63, 83, 86, 105, 153–54, 186
cover 5, 6, 8, 9, 12, 38, 53, 68, 70, 72, 79–81, 83, 86, 88–90, 94, 96–7, 98, 111, 115, 139, 143, 144, 185, 194–5
 cost of 3, 9, 48, 74, 80, 98, 111, 153, 154, 194
 cover sheet/log 5, 80, 84, 90, 194
 internal 1, 57, 72, 76, 81, 91, 92, 114, 168, 194
Croydon, London Borough 132, 136
curriculum 6, 93, 105
 coordinator 2, 69, 83, 143

development 69, 70, 109, 110, 112, 129, 168, 169
enrichment 10, 112
primary 112, 116
secondary 69, 93, 140
sixth form 71, 194
Subjects: art 115; business studies 69; CDT 69, 89, 93, 104, 113; drama 93; English 104, 131; E2L 108; French 69; geography 69, 104, 113, 115; history 69, 93, 104, 113; I.T. 69; mathematics 69, 131, modern languages 89, 93, 94, 106, 125, 126; music 69, 93, 113; P.E. 69, 93; science 69, 98–103, 125, 131

Davies, B. 47, 64
data bases: LEA 154, 185
 school 84
Davis, F. 45, 64
deprofessionalization 105, 173
Department for Education — School Teachers' Pay and Conditions Document 97, 107, 194–5
DES 4, 11, 124, 150, 155, 170, 179
Devon Education Department 132, 136
Department for Education 119, 178
differentiation 69, 102, 116, 158
discipline 21, 75, 88, 92, 93, 102, 116
discontinuity 3, 81, 89, 169, 183, 186
disruption 11, 70, 112, 114, 115, 139
disturbance 101, 139, 140, 141, 183
diversity 57
domestic responsibilities ix, 7, 28, 54, 146
Dunham, J. 2, 12

Earley, P. 4, 5, 11, 12, 44, 64, 85, 106, 107, 115, 120, 139, 140,

199

Index

142, 144, 147, 154, 155, 172, 178
East Sussex Education Department 132, 136
Ecob, E. 156
Educational change 128–132
Education-industry links 25, 71
efficiency 175, 177, 185
employment 6, 8, 9, 10, 92
   contract 1, 12, 53–4, 104–5, 112, 117, 160, 162, 167, 168, 174, 182
   flexible 80, 112, 170, 190, 192
   jobshare 40, 190, 192
   non-teaching staff 77, 97, 123, 173
   part-time ix, 1, 7, 75, 90, 104, 112, 146, 175, 189
   permanent 3, 7, 75, 83, 91–2, 192
   professional groups 158
   relationship xi, 9, 90, 157–162, 163, 175
   subsidiary/supplementary 34, 58, 86, 103
   supply teachers 1, 40, 72, 75, 80, 86, 90, 96, 97, 106, 109, 112, 114, 115, 195 (*see* separate listing)
   teachers (*see* separate listing) 75, 83, 91–2
equal opportunities 26, 117, 119
Esland, G. 143, 155
evaluation, 69, 71, 99
Evans, L. 64
Evetts, J. 145, 156
examination groups 94, 96
expectations of supply teachers 47–53, 62, 75, 77, 117, 127, 129, 139, 141–42, 144
   of pupils 100–1, 104
experience vii, ix, 8, 9, 10, 69, 100, 116, 118, 119, 169, 172, 192
Eyles, W. 175, 179

family commitments ix, 5, 7, 74, 86, 102, 104, 114, 115, 125, 178, 190, 193
feedback 81, 129–130
feminist research 7–8, 11, 28–9
flexibility 48, 51, 73, 77, 112, 118, 125, 142, 144
freelance 10, 115, 132, 133, 134, 182
Finch, J. 27, 28, 29, 30

G.C.S.E. xii, 79, 80, 94, 104, 124
G.E.S.T. xii, 2, 3, 9, 10, 40, 69, 74, 80, 134, 145, 150, 152, 183
Galloway, S. x, 11, 12, 43, 45, 64, 69, 82–107, 139, 154, 155, 156, 167, 168, 178, 179, 186, 188, 196
gender vii, ix, 5–8, 46–7, 105, 115, 142, 146–7, 178, 185, 186
Goffman, E. 45, 64
Goodson, I.
Grace, G. 157, 179
Great Britain House of Commons Interim Advisory Committee 3, 12, 167, 179
Great Britain House of Commons Committee on Science, Education 3, 12, 167
Green, K. 23, 30, 145

H.M.I. 4, 141, 156
Hackett, G. 11, 85, 106
Hammersley, M. 186, 188
Hargreaves, A. 7, 12
Hargreaves, D. 7, 12
Harré, R.C. 47, 64
Hassard, J. 139, 156
Hawes, W.R. 180
headteachers 9, 68–81, 88, 108–20, 132, 195
   reports for: 37–8
   views: 50–3
   survey comments: 144

Index

Hufferdine, J. 85, 107, 146, 156
Hughes, E. 43, 64, 143, 144, 156
Hulme, J. 4, 12, 43, 85, 107
humour 77, 80, 99, 102

identities 5, 9–10, 43–5, 55–7, 61–3, 103–5, 184
illness vii, 2, 8, 9, 72, 76, 79, 88, 89, 90, 110, 111, 114, 175, 178
image ix, 77, 119, 141
industrial action 97
information and checklists for supply teachers 32, 33, 77, 78, 126–27, 128, 131, 132, 173, 184, 185
INSET (*see* under Training)
instructors 89
insurance 72, 87, 111, 120, 178, 183
Interim Advisory Committee on School Teachers Pay and Conditions (*see* Great Britain) 152, 156
interviewing as research method 5, 8, 17–8, 99
invisibility viii, 6, 44, 50, 61–2, 84, 86, 91, 92, 100, 105, 106
Isle of Wight LEA 132, 136
isolation 32, 45, 48, 56, 61, 62, 99, 142

James, M. 70, 81
job content xi, 93, 103, 164, 165, 166, 168, 177
job satisfaction 5, 73, 112, 113, 157, 158
job security 3, 9, 105, 112, 175
job share (*see* employment)
Johnson, Y. 34, 41

Keep, E. 170, 171, 179
King, R. 7, 12
KITs xii, 32, 39, 40, 124, 127, 129, 130, 131, 134
Knight, C. 9, 196

labour markets 9–10, 15, 152, 184
  functional relocation xi, 159, 160, 177
  internal/external xi, 9, 53, 145, 157, 161, 168
  internalization/externalization 160, 162, 164, 177
  labour flexibility 153–54, 158
  labour shortages 161
  part-time work 9, 160
  professional 171, 172
  relocation
Lacey, C. 7, 12
latent conflict 6, 85, 86
Lawn, M. 157, 179
Leighton, P. 83, 107, 170, 179
Leverhulme Trust x, 11, 63, 106, 155
Lewis, D. 156
Lindley, R.M. 9, 83, 163, 196
Local Education Authorities x, xii, 2
  casual register/supply lists 34, 44, 52, 57, 74, 89, 90, 91, 92, 123, 129, 130, 149, 190
  central staff agencies (Birmingham) 115, 117, 120
  links to support groups 32–7
  power 138, 160, 170
  role of vii, 2, 3, 4, 8, 10, 31, 35, 36, 74, 86, 108, 110, 119, 122–135, 138, 160, 165, 176, 177, 182–83, 185
  supply pool 91, 143, 189
  supply teams 1, 3, 44, 52–53, 57, 86, 91, 115, 116, 143–44, 148, 150, 151–52
  systems 44, 52–3, 82, 123, 125, 147–52, 170, 187
local financial management 151, 154
Local Management of Schools 2, 79, 80, 110–11, 114, 123, 132–35, 133, 169, 178
Loveys, M. 4, 12, 44, 64, 107, 141, 146, 156

201

Index

Lukes, S. 6, 12, 85, 86, 107, 152, 156, 186, 188

Mackay, C. 179
Mandeville School 68–81, 194–5
 Mandeville Liaison Group 69
 teaching staff cover policy 9, 72, 79, 81, 194–5
Manpower Services Commission 124
Martin, J. 146, 156
Maughan, B. 156
McBride, R. 2, 12
mediocrity 62
Medshire 82, 86–7
mismatches 123, 148 (*see* also compatibility)
McCormick, R. 70, 81
Mead, G.H. 45, 64
Measor, L. 43, 65
Mellor, S. 134, 136
Millward, N. 179, 180
Milton Keynes Supply Teachers' Support Group:
 growth and development 31–35
 guide for supply teachers 34
 media interest 34
 relations with LEA 33
Morrison, M. 6, 9, 11–2, 44, 45, 64, 83, 96, 106, 107, 142, 145, 146, 153, 154, 155, 156, 175, 178, 180, 186, 188, 196
Mortimore, P. 140, 156
motherhood 17, 20, 145
Mullett, M. 4, 8, 12, 34, 35, 40, 42, 145, 156, 197
 survey research 12, 35–7, 189–193

naming of pupils 103–4
 of teachers 99–100, 104
National Curriculum 2, 3, 33, 35, 38, 50, 51, 58, 73, 109, 113, 117, 119, 129, 131–132, 148, 182, 191–3
national policy 182, 183, 184

National Primary Centre 69
Neill, S.R. St. J. 64
newsletters 3, 39, 125
Newton, M.J. 9, 11, 70, 81, 106, 197
Nias, D.J. 5, 12, 43, 45, 56, 63, 64, 142, 156
non-contact time 73, 80, 84, 97, 112, 185
non-teaching staff 77, 97, 123, 173
Norfolk LEA 132, 136

Oakley, A. 28, 29, 30
observation 6, 93, 98–105, 119
occupations xi, 5, 103, 164–5
occupational mobility 12, 161, 162, 175
organizational structure 160, 169, 175, 176, 177
Ouston, J. 156
Ozga, J. 12, 107

Packwood, A. 64
parents 88
 perspectives 21–3
pay and conditions 2–4, 16, 53–4, 56–7, 72, 74, 78, 92, 94, 115, 117, 143–44, 146, 148, 153, 176, 182, 194–5
Platt, J. 28, 30
power 6, 11, 12, 85, 105, 143, 152, 157, 164, 170, 171, 175, 181, 186, 187
practical work 93, 99, 100, 103
professionalism and professionalization ix, 4, 6, 8–10, 119, 139, 146–47, 168–79, 186, 187, 192
professional development 3, 8, 16, 24–5, 87, 105, 117, 119, 145, 184, 186, 192
proletarianization 166
pupils 2, 4, 69, 88, 94, 98–103, 104, 109, 127, 185

Index

pupils' learning vii, ix, 7, 9–11, 69, 70, 76, 94, 95, 103, 108, 109, 112, 115, 116, 130, 140, 190, 191

qualifications 1, 103, 149–50, 163, 165, 171, 174, 176, 192
quality ix, 2, 48, 49, 52, 53, 72, 75, 80, 96, 111, 115, 116, 119, 140, 142, 144–46, 148, 153, 157, 169, 173, 177, 189

rationalization 152, 153
Records of Achievement xii, 71, 72, 89, 98
recruitment and retention vii, 26, 37, 38, 118, 167, 168, 169, 175, 176, 193
redeployment 138, 144
redundancy 148, 151
research methodology 5–8, 10, 27–9, 181, 186
resources 77, 125, 131, 170
returners ix, 3–4, 8–11, 17, 38, 133, 145, 150, 175, 184, 186, 192
retirement and retired teachers 89, 91, 114, 115, 138, 148, 151, 186
Riseborough, G. 61, 64
Roberts, C. 146, 156
Roberts, H. 28, 30
Rose, J. 140, 155
Rutter, M. 140, 156
Ryan, P. 164, 179, 180

S.A.C.R.E. xii, 79
Safety issues 93
Salaman, G. 44, 65, 155
Sammon, P. 156
Sanday, A. 140, 156
Sandwell LEA 132, 136
Saran, R. 107, 179, 180
school
  budget 4, 9, 10, 16, 68, 80, 86, 98, 108–14, 116–18, 133, 158, 169, 170, 176, 182, 183
  buildings 72, 78, 84, 87, 97, 109, 194
  departments 70, 72, 76, 89, 90, 92, 96, 167, 194
  development plan 87
  employing organization 160, 169, 190, 193
  intake 87, 109
  leadership 140
  location 87, 108, 113, 117
  organization vii, xi, 6–8, 50, 58, 68, 72, 73, 77, 84, 85, 90, 96, 105, 138, 139, 140, 145, 166, 168, 183, 185, 186, 190, 194
  policies 26, 71, 79, 105–6, 133, 185, 194
  site 84, 89, 96, 104
  supply co-ordinators 74, 78, 79, 81, 82–108, 185, 194
  supply list 57, 59, 70, 74, 78, 109, 110, 114, 129, 130
  time 57, 138–9, 185
School types 128, 131
  clusters 4, 113, 122, 185, 189, 191
  infant 108–20
  inner city 9, 10, 108, 116
  primary 8, 75, 87, 123, 125, 139, 191
  rural 123, 127
  secondary 5, 8, 11, 82–107, 124, 125, 139
  special 75, 76
  small 126, 183
school governing bodies 26
School Teachers Review Body 4, 13
secondment 71, 119
self and self-image 43, 44, 45–6, 53–6, 61, 63, 142
self esteem 112, 129, 130
self supported study 2
setting work 93–5, 102, 104, 194
Shilling, C. 5, 12, 13, 43, 56, 65, 85, 107, 173, 176, 180

203

Index

shortages 3, 11, 40, 123–24, 173, 176, 183
significant others 45, 46, 63
Sikes, P. 43, 65
Simons, H. 27, 30
Smart, D. 180
Smith, A. 156
Speakman, M. 155
split classes 48, 59, 109, 168
staff development xi, 68, 74, 87, 90, 165
staff meeting 117
staff turnover 141
status 10, 100, 128, 134, 181, 184, 189
Stenning, R. 83, 107, 152, 153, 154, 156, 180
stereotypes ix, 46–7, 53, 185
Stevens, J. 160, 179
Stevens, M. 179, 180
Stoll, L. 156
stress 2, 12, 47, 51, 52, 72, 80, 90, 96
supply teachers vii, ix, x, 5, 6, 11, 69, 99, 167, 169, 189
  age 190, 192
  male/female ix, 7, 46, 98–105, 190, 192
  motivation vii, 4, 5, 54, 103, 190, 125, 184
  personal experience 8, 29–30, 56, 125, 175, 181, 190, 104–5
  personal qualities 25, 62, 99–100, 105, 144, 175
  resources 59, 60, 186, 190–193
  travel 89, 92, 96, 104, 191
  work schedules 49
supply teaching viii, 1, 10, 11, 98–105, 175, 189, 193
  costs 98, 133, 144
  duties 117
  experience 69, 100, 116, 118, 119, 125, 127, 133, 190
  familiarity with school 38, 48, 59, 70, 71, 73, 92, 98, 100, 110, 112, 114, 191
  with pupils 5, 70, 72, 99, 100, 104–5, 191
  general expertise 8, 76, 89, 92, 93, 103, 105, 128, 131, 139, 140, 184, 185
  payment 2, 72, 74, 78, 92, 115, 117, 143–44
  skills 2, 10, 49, 55–56, 62, 70, 75, 95, 92, 99, 104–5, 112, 116, 118, 128, 130, 144, 169, 183, 184, 191
  specialist expertise 8, 9, 70, 74, 76, 89, 90, 92, 94–6, 98, 102, 103, 105, 106, 109, 113, 131, 140, 168
  strategies 5, 54, 55, 58–62, 75, 77, 99, 101–4, 140
support groups 4, 8, 10, 131, 132, 135, 145, 182, 190, 191, 192
survey research 8, 35–7, 189–193
survival strategies 62, 94
symbolic interactionism 7, 43, 35

Teaching as a Career Initiative xii, 133
T.V.E.I. 2, xii, 79, 80, 124
teacher absence vii, 2, 44, 47, 62, 72, 76, 79, 80, 82, 87, 88, 90, 94, 95, 98, 100, 108, 110, 112, 116, 120, 138, 183, 194
teacher morale 9, 79, 82, 84, 97
teacher release 69, 79, 124
time 3, 6, 55, 56, 62, 69, 70–2, 78, 80, 85, 90, 95, 104, 108–10, 112, 126–27, 138–39, 185, 186, 187
timetable 70, 76, 77, 79, 84, 89, 94, 98
Times Educational Supplement 11, 34
teachers
  advisory 9, 108, 119
  'associate' 117
  inactive 91, 122, 123

Index

part-time 3, 5, 53, 112, 143, 189
permanent 9, 10, 12, 46–50, 115, 140, 168, 192–193
supply (*see* separate listing)
unemployed 115
student 109
support 109, 112
teaching appointments and interviews 4, 8, 10, 16, 25–7, 123, 130, 150, 178
teacher associations (AMMA, NAHT, NASUWT, NUT, PAT, SHA) x, 4, 11, 139, 142, 155, 148
teacher supply 4, 11, 35, 123, 132, 135, 139, 147, 167, 173, 176, 182
teaching work-force viii, 11, 91–2, 153–54, 123, 193
team teaching 140
Trafford, V. 107, 179, 180
training 2, 6, 9, 29–30, 83, 89, 119, 162, 163, 165, 169, 172, 174, 177, 178, 189, 191, 194
  employer-based 161–2
  for governors 26, 40
  for supply teachers 3, 4, 8, 10, 17, 39, 57, 73, 74, 116, 119, 120, 124, 127, 129, 131, 132, 134, 135, 142, 149, 150, 154, 184, 185, 186
  for the National Curriculum 35, 148
  for women returners 119, 124, 150
  initial teacher training xii, 19, 26, 79, 80, 89, 103, 165, 176, 190
  initial training 132, 163
  investment in 162–3, 165, 176
  general 29–30, 122, 134, 139, 148, 154
  school-based 74, 79, 90, 118, 165
  INSET and in-service training ix, xi, xii, 2, 4, 5, 9, 10, 12, 44, 47, 50, 52, 69, 71, 73, 74, 79, 84, 88, 90, 91, 103, 110, 111, 113, 114, 117, 118, 124, 174, 176, 189, 191
Trotter, A. 5, 13, 44, 65, 85, 107, 175, 180

underclass 144

values 45, 62, 128
visibility x, 6, 45, 82, 86, 91, 92, 100, 106, 183, 187
voluntary work 6, 24, 104, 125, 133

Welcome pack 77 (*see also* checklists and information for supply teachers)
West Sussex LEA 9, 122, 128, 132, 135
Wolverhampton LEA 132, 136
Woodhead, C. 140, 155
Woods, P. 43, 62, 65
work vii, viii, ix, 6, 9, 12, 31–2, 43, 44, 45, 86, 93, 106, 143, 183, 190, 191
work experience 109
work sheets 49, 99, 101, 104, 116, 194
work shadowing 126
work loads 48, 58
Wragg, E. 5, 13, 44, 65, 85, 107, 175, 180

youth work 104